Transformation in Transition

A Memoir

George Coleridge-Taylor

Sierra Leonean Writers Series

Transformation in Transition

Sierra Leonean Writers Series (SLWS)
Warima/Freetown/Accra
120 Kissy Road, Freetown, Sierra Leone
Publisher: Prof. Osman Sankoh (Mallam O.)
publisher@sl-writers-series.org

SLWS Series on
Public Policy and Public Service

Development needs effective institutions and public policies. Many of Sierra Leone's problems can be traced to public policy failures and lack of probity in the governance of public institutions. The SLWS Series on "Public Policy and Public Service" aims to tackle these issues by providing scholars and practitioners a platform to document their experiences, ideas and research findings. It will advance knowledge on how public policies are made, their effects on development and wellbeing, and the different ways institutions, citizen activism and private interests influence the content and effectiveness of public policies. This is a Series for those who want to share their knowledge on how public institutions function and how sound and effective policies can improve the lives of Sierra Leoneans. Informed bureaucrats, policy makers, politicians, legal practitioners, social activists, journalists and academics are encouraged to submit manuscripts. The Series publishes three kinds of books: personal reflections or memoirs; collection of think pieces or short essays; and research manuscripts.

Titles include:

George Coleridge-Taylor
TRANSFORMATION IN TRANSITION

Yusuf Bangura
DEVELOPMENT, DEMOCRACY AND COHESION: CRITICAL ESSAYS WITH INSIGHTS ON SIERRA LEONE AND WIDER AFRICA CONTEXTS

Lansana Gberie
WAR, POLITICS AND JUSTICE IN WEST AFRICA: ESSAYS FROM 2003-2014

Andrew Keili
PONDER MY THOUGHTS (Vol. 1)

Sama Banya
LOOKING BACK: MY LIFE AND TIMES

Ebenezer Solo Collier
PRIMARY AND SECONDARY EDUCATION IN SIERRA
LEONE: EVALUATION OF MORE THAN 50 YEARS OF
PRACTICES AND POLICIES

Dedication

- To my late mother, "Sissy Alice":
  Whose loving hands guided my infant fingers in producing the letters of the alphabet.

- To Aunty Elachie (Nurse Hilda):
  Whose loving care followed after my mother.

- To Mama Telay:
  Whose contribution launched my transformation.

- To my dad:
  For encouragement through difficult times.

- To my maternal Uncle George:
  Whose confidence and constant support in difficult times were inspiring.

Appreciation

The idea for this product was driven into me by various friends and colleagues and not only did it take a long time to germinate, it has taken even longer to be finalised because of my other preoccupations in church and masonic engagements and bouts of illness.

I select for special mention and appreciation Professor Eldred Durosimi Jones, whose meticulous and expert guidance during my undergraduate studies in English Language and Literature inspired me and has sustained my interest to the present. I continue to treasure his acceptance of me as his protégé and I assure him that, on my part, he will continue to be my special and revered mentor.

I hope that all those who have waited patiently for this work will find it worthwhile.

Special thanks are due to those who exerted themselves in the laborious task of typing from my horrible writing as a labour of love: Martha Georgina, who typed the first few pages, and Aminata, for the first draft. Special appreciation is also due to George Christo-Baker, who typed the second draft alone, and Dr. Nemata Majeks-Walker, who edited with me and finalised the typing of the entire manuscript.

Tribute to Professor Clifford Nelson-Fyle

It would be a disservice to true friendship if I fail to acknowledge the contribution of Professor Clifford Nelson-Fyle to my retirement years. Caught between the abrupt end to my "Democracy" years and the gaping future of professional idleness, he invited me to join his LEKON Consultancy. His was an indigenous company producing indigenous language books for nationwide use whilst simultaneously undertaking Human Resource Training in Inter-Personal Relations and Business Communications Skills. Our interaction with top-level administrators in elite corporations and banks was as beneficial to us professionally as to them. For me personally, it was gratifying to be sought after professionally by a former distinguished Head of the UN Indigenous Languages for Africa Programme, co-author with Professor Eldred Jones of the first Krio Dictionary and author of the Sierra Leone National Anthem.

May his Soul Rest in Elysium.

A Review by Dr. Mrs. Nemata Majeks-Walker

Written in beautiful and lively prose, *Transformation in Transition* is a stimulating story of Mr. George Coleridge-Taylor's childhood in Freetown, his university education at Fourah Bay College in Sierra Leone and Durham in the UK where he excelled in the art of debating, and his work in public service. The book vividly depicts his experiences as professional head of the Sierra Leone Diplomatic Service, Special Executive Assistant to the President, Head of the University's Philosophy Department, and Chair of the National Tourist Board and the National Commission for Democracy and Human Rights. It portrays some of the opportunities and challenges he experienced at various levels in the civil service, the public service, academia and the wider society in which he was engaged. The International Community features prominently as the author reveals activities in his various Foreign Service assignments and as head of the Foreign Service.

Contents

1

Transformation in Transition

I think of transition as a physical phenomenon, which fundamentally involves physical movement as opposed to transformation, which is essentially mental. The former indicates the various changes of external status or other circumstances that together constitute the environment through and within which life experiences unfold, and change for good or ill.

As we traverse these pits and pinnacles of change, our identity is enlarged or diminished through a combination of nature, nurture and the chemistry injected by the individual will. This is transformation, and the crucial factor is the individual will. Like transition, it is also a process of change, but transformation is more spiritual and lasting and reveals the defining features that identify us as greater or lesser human beings.

This preamble sets the stage for the story of my own life as a blend of transition and transformation.

2
In the Beginning

I was born in a generation when every baby in the then colony area of Salone was assigned at birth into a social stratum defined by its parentage. You discovered later in life that you were either super class (aristocrat), upper middle class, lower middle class or among the lower classes.

My situation was rather enigmatic because my parentage had not developed a substantial identity in the elite professions (e.g. legal or academic), which were a major qualification for inclusion in the aristocratic or upper middle class. Although my paternal grandfather was a medical doctor, he did not make a significant impact locally before migrating to The Gambia and there is no trace of his return. Of course, being born on 4 July made me a bit special and entitled me in later years to special treatment at American Government Independent Day Celebrations. That was at a later stage during my transition.

Although the pedigree was not star studded, it did contain a pearl or two. The Taylor Family of Ibo Town, Waterloo Village consisted of three brothers – Daniel, Emmanuel and Samuel. These were our grandparents. My grandfather, Dan, was the illustrious favourite who went to England, qualified as a medical doctor, married an English lady and bore the musical prodigy Samuel Coleridge-Taylor, whose middle name, Coleridge, my father promptly annexed to ours for family and national pride.

The family name of Coleridge-Taylor has remained only in our branch of the tree in Sierra Leone. For me it was a source of inspiration and a challenge. Sustaining an existing aristocracy only required conformity and consistency; establishing one was much more demanding – and that was how I envisaged my mission.

Through my mother of blessed memory, I inherited one fourth of my identity from Mende land. My grandparents on my father's side were full-blooded Krios of Ibo and Yoruba descent with Taylor and Williams Krio names. My maternal granddad, George Sawyer, was of similar origin, but fired by the Ibo obsession with trade, he had migrated (also from Waterloo) to the Torma Bum and Medina Chiefdoms in the hinterland where he established trading posts as a "factor" exporting piassava, cacao, and other products,, and became a local "Dr. Livingstone". Being the local aristocrat, PC Chief Nuni's Cousin, Madam Mary Marsh, was given to him in marriage. He promptly dispatched their two children, George and Alice, to Freetown for education and Krio upbringing. Thus was my Mende umbilical cord severed, except for a familiarisation tour to which I was treated as a seven-year old boy.

My childhood was spiced with a few interesting peculiarities. My friends, playmates and other contemporaries could only boast of four grandparents – two paternal and two maternal. I had five, i.e. two grandfathers and three grandmothers. Mary Marsh on my maternal side was singular. She was the cousin of a Paramount Chief, very conservative and somewhat aloof. Marriage to a young successful Freetown businessman was for her a pleasant experience as long as he was 'Lord of the manor' in Victoria, Torma Bum and Sulima area, buying and exporting palm kernels, cacao, piassava etc. Their two children, Alice, my mother, and George, climaxed her marital life but she detached herself from George Sawyer (Senior) when the polygamous temptation of the vicinity began to distract him. As a truly loving mother, however, she consented that he

3

should bring both children to Freetown for their education. I am the product of that decision.

I recall our first meeting when I was old enough to recognise and appreciate her. There were, of course, earlier visits when I must have enjoyed the cuddling that is the natural right of every grandchild. How I sorrow for those who, for all sorts of regrettable reasons, are deprived of that joyful experience. May the joy of a grandparent's cuddling be the lot of children everywhere.

On that first conscious visit I mentioned above, I had become an investigative little boy and curiously observed the extraction of palm oil from the fruit. I mischievously conjured up visions of myself immersed in a large cask of cool palm oil but was soon jolted into reality, remembering what happened to cockroaches that dared to bath in bottles of palm oil.

On another occasion, my curiosity had an unexpected destabilising effect on all and sundry, especially my "Sissy Alice", and granny Mary. Strolling across our compound, I noticed a gigantic bowl of what appeared to be milk. Propelled by curiosity rather than greed, I plunged my thick, forefinger in, licked, sucked and behold, I had never tasted anything sweeter in my whole life. It was irresistible. Relying on the indulgent protection of my mother and grandma, I began to swallow the lot and must have fallen asleep even before finishing it. After about 36 hours of unbroken sleep, I woke up and drowsily found myself surrounded by pairs of anxious eyes, tearfully between ecstasy and anxiety. The room was clouded in some herbal smoke, which must have choked me into waking up – assisted as I was told by some friendly biting of my 'big toe'. As I discovered later, the powerful potion was the bamboo palm wine, known as 'duvui', which is considered the most potent natural alcohol drink in our part of the world. After that childhood episode, it took me years to taste alcohol again, when as a customs officer and later as diplomat, it was almost a professional requirement.

Oh dear, I almost lost track of my other two grandmothers. These are, on my father's side, two sisters like two peas in a pod. By coincidence, one was Mary, like the maternal counterpart, and the other was Margaret, my dad's mother. The sisters were not so identical in attitude but somehow we the kids saw them as a unity. They were always together, in consultation and very tactful at frustrating the children's strategy of divide and rule. A request denied in camp A was certain to fail in camp B. There was no appellate mechanism.

In the attempt to rescue me from the supposed stifling of my manhood tendency by an over indulgent mother, I was billeted to the camp of my grandaunt Mary – Camp A – which turned out to be a civilian 'guard room' in military terms. Being the only child in the house (aged 6-7 years), with no playmate in my age group, and under strict and constant supervision, infant school became a welcome daily escape and a happy respite. Little wonder then that education released and nourished me into the person I became.

I have to admit there was a silver lining to my cloud at camp A, located at Fifth Street. Being located a stone's throw from Regent Road, which was the convergence of most activities in the "Baimbrace" community, there was always an opportunity to escape into the wider and wilder world. We were three inmates in the house, but I was the preferred and realistically the only handy bag about the home. My cousin, Gladys (aka Baykay), was then in the budding stages of young adulthood about 19 to 20 years – and used every occasion to behave like the latter. She was very kind and considerate, always ready to protect me from the wrath (provoked or otherwise) of the commandant. In return, I had to run all her many errands, which I enjoyed tremendously, partly because of the temporary escape but also in view of the material benefit which I invariably gained. Her love of sweets was ever to my advantage. She had an insatiable appetite for changing balls – a ball shaped candy, which changed into various colours as the unrelenting tongue rolled around it.

In competing demand was "New cream toffee" – a delicious blend of chocolate and sugar candy, deliciously dear to every palate because it resisted every attempt to reduce it in size by chewing as it melted ever so slowly around the impatient teeth and appreciative tongue.

My bonus was that because of my frequent visits, the most popular vendor of these sweets had listed me as a favorite customer and I was always welcomed with an indulgent smile whilst my dream was rewarded with modest additions to my purchases, designated as my personal gifts.

As a bidding middleman, I soon acquired, under my agent/cousin's tuition, a few skills above the level of my age groups. I was taught to observe, without detection, the appearance of a certain young man in the vicinity, report discreetly but promptly to my "principal" and be prepared to relay any communication with dispatch and all the while looking like the innocent flower. The reward was two-fold. Initially, an extra portion in my luncheon or dinner bowl was sufficient for a voracious lad. Actually, my rewards were unsolicited and unexpected but ever so welcome – especially the regular pocket change (a glittering penny) I got from my cousin's boyfriend. I never realised I was doing him any favour except reporting his arrival but he must have known how much my services were worth to him. In later years, with the added wisdom derived from seven active daughters, I came to realise how much I had learnt about the intricate workings of a young damsel's mind. The older ones must have noticed this when they nicknamed me "SAVO".

The Camp A era of my young life ended abruptly in November 1940 when my Camp B grandma, Margaret, died and the three of us were relocated to Circular Road. Our new compound was distinguished by a gigantic breadfruit tree, which was a landmark for strangers seeking direction and an attraction to hungry folk around. For us within the compound, it was almost a gold mine.

Apart from the Taylor-Pearce compound, a few hundred yards up the road, there was hardly another competing breadfruit tree that provided such delicious varieties – breadfruit fried, roasted, boiled, oven-baked; and prepared as chips, flour, palm oil porridge (locally known as Ebe) and above all, chewing gum from its fluid. I recall Robinson Crusoe glorifying the coconut plant for providing food and drink at the same tree. The breadfruit would have been a picnic package.

Our new home was blessed with the presence of my favorite aunty, Elachie. She was known outside the home as Nurse Hilda – an aspect reflected in her kindly nature. Her two daughters, Ola and Pattie, who were in my age group, became my domestic playmates but, once again, I was the only juvenile male in the household, performing appropriate chores like publicly disposing of garbage, a task that the 'ladies' were very anxious to avoid. However, the environment exposed me to some unfamiliar feminine games like skipping through a rope being swung above and below you by a girl on each side of you; mock food preparation, known as play cook, using grass as vegetable, tomato and milk tins as pots. The play cook is climaxed by a mode of consumption in which the food is held under one's chin accompanied by a clucking sound like a hen calling to her chicks.

All of these diversions were peculiarly feminine but I learnt to adjust and eventually enjoyed them. My special respite was the occasional mock marriage, when I assumed the masculine role of husband, was put in charge, and pampered as real husbands were in those days.

An exciting aspect of my boyhood was the regular holiday trip to my grandpa, who had returned to Waterloo on his retirement from the produce exporting business. My mother and I would stop over at all the villages between Allen Town and Waterloo and it turned out that we had relations all along the route. Apparently, they all pampered me because they thought I was a good pupil. This meant I was given the freedom of the compound- - free to climb or otherwise attack any fruit tree to satisfy my voracious appetite and take left over with me on our departure. Even my local cousins benefited from my visits as there were fewer restrictions on their recreation in order to accommodate me. It was hospitality at its best.

On arrival at Waterloo, I felt I was transported into the world of storybooks. Lush vegetation welcomed me to a fairy-tale wonderland, imaginary castles, caves and who-knows-what, gigantic mango trees with their luscious foliage and bewitching aroma that filled your nostrils before the tongue could intrude.

Since my parents were not together, my dad never accompanied me on these trips. This made me more relaxed as I saw him as a stern, restrictive disciplinarian. In any case, I did not miss him, as I had already been consigned and adjusted to the gentler inclinations of my doting mum; my aunt Hilda, with her tendency of the gentle nurse; and the indulgence of my elder female cousins, with their special interests in their favourite messenger. As for my contemporary female cousins, they competed in pampering me, being the mini-macho character around. There were, of course, contestants for this latter position, like Kasho Wellington next door, but I was home grown and home based.

My dad featured prominently particularly over education and the church choir practice, when discipline was an absolute norm. Bless him for those early days. A bit of the rod really hurt but its effect was more lasting as a lifetime deterrent, complementing the precepts and examples of elders.

As the only child of my mother for 15 long years, I was idolised; in addition to me, her only other passion was her job as an infant and primary schoolteacher.

In that environment, I developed a love for education very early – especially for reading and writing. The thrill of those feminine fingers over mine rounding my O and positioning my K as though ready to kick a ball or take a stroll is still alive in me.

Out of genuine concern or jealousy – I still cannot decide - my paternal aunt and guardians felt I was too attached and becoming effeminate and spoilt, and so we were separated. Ironically, I found myself in an environment that could hardly have been more feminine. All my cousins were girls and took special pleasure in teaching me to skip and play the hand clapping and hopping girls' game called "Accra". To this day, I cannot fathom why it is so called; perhaps and only perhaps, it was imported from Ghana.

To sustain my masculinity, I used every opportunity out of the feminine domestic environment to indulge in barefoot football, for which no formal pitch or statutory venue was required. A wide footpath, with little or no traffic or a school / church compound was ideal for a 4 to 6 a side. There were also more technical exploits like the "coaxing", which involved hopping on one foot, while the other kicked, caught and cushioned a squeezed out orange without interruption up to 100 or more hops. This highly competitive game encouraged choirboys to arrive for the church choir practice well ahead of the designated time. Ajayi Robinson was my champion competitor.

Upon reflection, the breathing accompanying contests gave our lungs excellent exercise in preparation for attacking emotional hymns as well as Handel classics, although this was far from our thoughts. Father Ephraim Robinson was the spiritual mentor of the Ebenezer Church Choir, its official Class Leader, and because of his advanced age and clerical demeanor, he was a virtual paterfamilias to that mixed bunch of angelic voices and known generally as "Pa Rob." Angelic certainly we were when it came to singing. Our patient organist, who eventually became a professor, at some time or the other, had an individual session with every chorister in polishing his minstrels.

Breathing, posture, voice control, transition from chest to head voice, and even the maximum distance between the lips were decreed with mathematical accuracy to produce the most mellifluous sounds. "Probay" was the convenient juvenile abbreviation for "probation", the first door through which we entered the sanctum sanctorum of the choir. This was an approximate period of one year, when you came to choir practice regularly and punctually, sat in a pew behind the choir stall, listened, learned and practised the art of humming softly, admired the symphonic blend of canines and cantories among the soprano ranks, but marveled the most at the mellifluous emission of the Leading treble, gently and generally distributed by the acoustic spirits. Here, at last, the mature listener is transported and lost in wonder, love and praise!! Inspiration was never in short supply to the probationer so that when it was time for his trial, after that apprenticeship which varied between 6 and 12 months, he was ready for initiation and absorption into the fold.

I have never known or heard of anyone who was refused absorption into the choir after a whole year's probation. If it happened, it would be such a sad blow to the victim and his family; of course, there could be the rare expulsion – but only for bad behavior, which the family could never live down.

In my father's family, singing was like a special gift. We were fanatical about choral music, with each of us constantly competing to be the lead singer and favourite soloist, be it soprano alto, tenor or bass.

Coming from a stolidly Christian background, my induction into the church choir was an inevitable rite of passage. Thankfully, it was a delightful experience. True to form, the men usually arrived half an hour after the appointed hour, whereas half an hour before practice time, we the boys converged at the church compound, which was also the school playing field. This provided us with a full hour of unrestrained recreation three evenings a week. Our gleeful exuberance did have its punctuation but only on Wednesday, when our choir class leader and spiritual mentor joined us for reflection and collection of church membership dues. Father Ephraim Robinson (aka Pa Rob) had the reputation of being one of the strictest disciplinarians at the Methodist Boys High School and, true to form, he always arrived at unspecified and unexpected hours, timed to interrupt our pranks and games--Talk of the mice scuttling when the cat arrived? Our shorthand code was "Pa Rob, Pa Rob!" On a fateful evening, the unfortunate among the mice happened to be me. Chasing the football, which bounced out of the field into the path of a car, I was nearly knocked down. Missed by a few centimetres, I found myself as I recovered my breath, staring into the approaching eyes of Pa Rob. "George", he said in a half whisper, "if your soul falls out, you would kick it before realizing it isn't a ball". I was relieved that my colleagues did not hear the remarks, from which a nickname would have certainly emerged. There were enough nicknames in circulation already and I already had one. There was no room for a second! Thoughtfully, he did not mention it during our Bible class, but he did caution us against playing too much and dangerously.

Oh, how I loved the choral experience, as singing was one of my most enjoyable activities. I was probably a bit vain as I often sang, because my voice drew continuous compliments from old and young alike. When E.D. Coker, who later became a music professor, selected Jabez Williams and me for special training, it was like a new session in the classroom. Learning to read musical notes, understanding clefs, octave and converting dots on lines into tonic solfa – notes was challenging but exciting. He even taught me how to produce the head voice while controlling the gap between my lips.

Soon my singing self-evolved into dimensions that captured the heavenly harmony of immortal composers like Bach, Handel, Mendelson and Beethoven; and although the only instrument I could strum was the ukelele, I was generous enough to myself to think I was a musician. After all, when I became not only the leader of the canines against the cantories but also the leading soprano in the choir, I suddenly discovered that singing was, in fact, a lucrative musical profession. Every time I rendered a solo in an anthem or an aria by itself, I earned enough pocket money from doting elders to conceal one third for my friends throughout the following week and still please the home with the balance.

When I joined the Ebenezer Methodist Church Choir at Circular Road, my father was already the leading baritone. It was probably an innovative experiment by the organist to pair father and son in a duet. Well, it proved more successful than any of us anticipated, and so by Divine grace and favour, I became the Lead soprano, normally labeled "First treble". In later years as a mature adult, I used to tell my dad he could be first bass whenever I travelled!! Sometimes I wonder why I did not devote myself to singing as a career.

In my soprano days, every solo attracted so many shillings into my pocket that if the effort and the returns had been sustained and commercialised I should be quite comfortable today. In my youthful years, singing was not a career option in Krio Society.

It was left to the "goombay" exponents like "Peter Na Lepet" and Ebenezer Kalendar to provide the regular musical menu at Krio festivities with the goombay and guitar string respectively. For the benefit of non-Krio readers "Peter Na Lepet" was pseudonym for a certain local band who specialised in drum syncopation accompanied by spicy Krio proverbs delivered in rhythmic songs and choruses. Dancing to that music was a real exercise in muscle control. The older men, their trousers held up by the inevitable braces, struggled frantically to loosen their arms by tilting their heads from side to side.

In contrast, the women, old and young, would engage in a competitive display of syncopated hip swinging. The beauty of this attraction is that the performers only see the other dancers. Since the emphasis is all *a posteriori*, the creaking old men and the onlookers derived all the pleasure.

I have been unable to know how Peter was given that pseudonym or whether it was appropriate. Literally, it means "Peter is a leopard" but our subject never seemed fearful or particularly courageous, although he was certainly a maestro in his performance.

Without realizing it at the time, I may have been drawn subconsciously to speaking, reading and literature generally by my obsession with singing. I could not help noting that hymns and anthems were actually beautiful poetry set to beautiful music. I soon began to visualise prose as elongated poetry. I have never quite abandoned that perception and in later years, I have regretted my inability to create for myself a fusion of the skills and sensibilities of Coleridge-Taylor and Taylor-Coleridge. Nevertheless, I have been truly enriched by the music of the former and the poetry of the latter.

During my earlier school days, music lessons outside the church choir were luxuries my family could not afford, as I was among the barefooted majority, whose day was devoted to working at school, church and home on a very tight schedule. Money was even tighter. Coleridge-Taylor's music was not even on my menu, but poetry was. I began with simple acrostics like "The Beggar"

> There, hungry, penniless, unfriended goes
> Honored not by the stones that kiss his toes
> Embracing, the epitome of woes.
> But he had once with riches been endowed.
> Enticed by fawning friends, for he was proud
> Gorgeous extravagance he lavished on the crowd.
> Gone are the those days, far far removed the date
> And now a tattered derelict of Fate
> Rags are his robes and dregs his treasured plate.

My growing love for the written and spoken word proved a blessing. I was fascinated by the mellifluous flow of rhymed couplets long before I could grasp the expanse of poetic interpretation. Pope and Dryden were prolific exponents of such poetry.

O simple man presume not God to scan
The proper study of mankind is man

However, my passion for words evolved from poems for the form IV Class magazine through competitive Literary and Debating Society Prizes, and the Rhetoric Society Prize at Fourah Bay College, where a linguistic maestro in the person of Dr. Eldred Durosimi Jones, then Head of the English Department, fine-tuned our talents. Deservedly, he now holds the position of Emeritus Professor.

3
School Days

My education had its earliest beginnings under the guiding hand of my dearly beloved mother, fondly known by all and sundry as "Sissy Alice". She was herself a kindergarten teacher and because I was very much Mama's pet and only child for 15 years, my kindergarten days were spent almost permanently by her side. Consequently, there was I always toying with pencil and crayon, either colouring pictures or laboriously trying to copy letters, figures and diagrams.

Even at the early age of 3-5 years, when my right arm stretched over my head could not touch my left ear, I must have been a mini strategist. One of my schemes of keeping my mum always at my elbow was by constantly seeking her assistance in holding my pencil correctly, matching
pictures to words and fighting with spellings and punctuation of two and three letter words. No wonder it took my darling Sissy fifteen long years to provide me with a sibling sister. I must have been that possessive without realising it.

The seed she planted in my mini brain seems to have germinated, as I found the Infants classes of Tabernacle school both pleasant and profitable. As I recall, the Infant school was between Kindergarten and Primary school. Probably because of being the smallest in the class, I was always seated in the front row and this put me directly under the watchful eye of the teacher. Ms. Martin was older than the others and a very caring but strict disciplinarian. Ms. Bright was shortish, aesthetic and reputed for dispensing punishment rather hastily. My favourite was Ms. Thompson, who later became Mrs. Lisk and one of my favourite infant recollections was being selected to present her with a bouquet and a brief recitation when she was about to get married.

Infant school was more pleasant because the pupils on either side of me – Nadette Metzger (later Mrs. Donald George) and Patricia Parker (Mrs. Ken During) -- were very nice and popular with the teachers and their popularity rubbed off on me. Because of my reading habit and my mother's professional attention, I was able to whisper answers when they were in doubt and these two fairy sisters would augment my paltry lunch in compensation. Such was my profit in Infant School.

Another exciting aspect of this level of education was our occasional opportunity of welcoming British Sailors from warships berthed in our harbour during the Second World War. If your name was top of the chart in Reading and Writing, you were bound to receive a souvenir, invariably a shining silvery penny with a hole in the center that could buy you loads of lunch at a farthing a piece for four days! Nadette Metzger and I were the usual beneficiaries.

Being promoted from Primary 3 to Standard 2 in Primary School (and skipping Standard 1) seemed like a herculean achievement, but it turned out to be a herculean task. Little did I imagine the number of assignments, the amount of homework or the ferocity of the punishment for the slightest infraction. No matter how hard you tried, or how small you were in stature, sympathy was the most excluded commodity in those classrooms. How does one give the answer to "3.5÷2.5" in two seconds, whilst confronted by an elevated cane waiting to descend on any part of your tender flesh?

Unlike "The Village School Master", we could not laugh with counterfeited glee at all his jokes, for not a joke had he. Sober, steadfast and austere was a more accurate description of each and all of our teachers. Leader of the pack was "D. J.

Bankole-Pearce Esq", learned in Maths, English, Greek, and Latin. We were introduced to the last two subjects after taking our entrance exams in Standard 6 for Secondary School admission. He was, of course, quite confident that none of his pupils would dare to fail. Passing through that special class with us (a year ahead) were pupils who became national luminaries like Francis Minah, Oredola Palmer, Alex Browne and Sama Banya. Modupeh Taylor-Pearce was my contemporary and closest friend, especially as we lived few doors apart. Indeed, most of our pupils did well enough to earn government scholarships to secondary schools in the days when your performance was the only qualification for a scholarship. Lest I forget, his lieutenants in the teaching and caning business were no less formidable. Therefore, Messrs. M. E. Peeler, M'Cormack, M. B. Jones and E. A. Coker deserve special mention and gratitude for keeping the fire burning while the dross fell from the gold. Lest I forget the painful price of forgetfulness in those days, I hasten to recall the daily pilgrimage to private lessons at Mr. Fyfe's residence, where another cane hovered perilously over us like a conductor's baton bereft of its soothing musical aura.

There was enough playfulness and kid glove treatment at Kindergarten and Infant School to make Primary School starting at Standard 1 look like a looming challenge. My elation of being catapulted to Standard 2 was only natural, but it only confronted me with a greater challenge. Totally unprepared for the change, I became a bit slowly drawn to Ebenezer Amalgamated School. Ebenezer was actually the name of the church whose basement was occupied by the school. I belong to both, and when I declare my Ebenezer identity, I sometimes have to explain that I attended Ebenezer Day School, Sunday School, Church and Choir, leading to my later positions of Education Committee chair, Class leader and Trustee. Living on the same street, Circular Road, completed my confinement.

Our teachers in Standard 2 seemed to appreciate that we were greenhorns from baby schools but had the stage set from the beginning to prepare us for the ordeal ahead. For a start, we had classes but no classrooms, except for Standard 6. In this educational amphitheater, we had a grandstand view of all that was to come – and what a foretaste it was! From Standard 3 to Standard 5, there was a weekly rotation of "hot mental" sessions, when the helpless students were expected, under the threat of an elevated whipping cane, to solve problems such as 3.5÷or x2.5 in less than five seconds; failing which the almighty rod descended with the speed and force of a thunderbolt. There was no advantage in working it out in anticipation of your turn because the question would invariably be changed before it reached you. However, we did learn from our seniors to soften the effect of the thunderbolt by padding our backs and bottoms with extra clothes or exercise books. If you were unlucky, however, the meteor might just landed on your arm or shoulder.

Incidentally, severe caning was never reported at home for fear of increased punishment. A case in point was the truant who was stretched around a concrete pillar by four stalwarts while the headmaster administered sixty merciless strokes. He reported the beating at home and fell ill for a few days. On his recovery, he was sent back by his parents with a recommendation for six more, generously dispensed and meekly absorbed.

Overall, competition was keen and healthy – and parents were really committed to advancing us. The result was that almost everyone went to private lessons after school. For us, this was an extra opportunity to be acquainted, fraternise, find time for 5-to-7 aside football matches, in any open space and generally sweat it out before returning home to do the school homework and the house chores. There was no time for resting but then, who needed it. We were young and energetic and rest was boring anyway.

Standard 6 was a world apart. This was the exit point from Primary School – and the standards were so high that many of the administrators who effectively managed the African colonial service up to independence were recruited from that level. In that final year, we were introduced to Greek and Latin and were prepared for the competitive scholarship to secondary schools offered by the government.

4
The Prince's Boys

I am not sure we had any golden glitter as we exited the crucible of Ebenezer Primary School, but perhaps we could have passed for half-polished brass at that ripe young average age of 12. Thus, we entered, in gleeful anticipation, the brave new world of the secondary school.

My first day at the Prince of Wales School was a turning point in my life. Everything seemed so strange and different from my previous experience. The end of childhood was at hand as the pleasures and responsibilities of teenage existence slowly and imperceptibly dawned upon me and other new entrants. It was a freshman's typical experience.

Our initial hurdle was the formation of new friendships. I realise on reflection that we treated everyone as a friend. Friends of old, mostly from the same school, were, of course, special. Alliances soon sorted themselves out, motivated by various links, such as common hobbies, academic interest, domestic proximity or family connection. My observation indicates that this was a common experience of every new boy and girl in secondary school in my day and I suspect that this is still the case.

This was in 1945 and the war was nearing its end but not yet over when we reclaimed the Prince of Wales School. As the admiralty had occupied our school building, we were enrolled at the Government Model School building at Circular Road in the heart of town. However, at the beginning of the next school year in 1946, we were lined up for the exodus from our temporary home to take our first glimpse of the legendary Prince of Wales building, whose

21

foundation stone was laid by HRH the Prince of Wales on 6 April, 1925.

The school at this time was beginning to admit Sixth Form pupils and it was such a wonder for diminutives like me to meet six footers like Oju Mends, Ransford During, Johny Patnelli, Arthur Stewart and Peche Betts, and see them as fellow pupils. They were particularly fearful as swimmers and known as sharks.

Some of us had been warned by our simplistic parents not to enter the sea (pond) bordering our school until we could swim. No one ever told us how or where we could learn! No pupil of the school ever remembered that admonition.

Although there was a modern swimming pool at Tower Hill, it was reserved for military personnel. For ordinary folk like ourselves, the only sight of water accessible to us was the odd stream, the standpipe for domestic use and the "Baimbrace" well, where social gossip was the favourite pastime. At home, swimming was left to wayward boys who strayed off to Susan's Bay and similar areas to brave the ocean. Inevitably, there were a number of tragic accidents, which restrained those of us who were obedient. Somehow, our common background made the prospect of collective swimming with friends under watchful eyes quite attractive. In preparation for the adventures, I made the strategic move of befriending the giants of the Sixth Form for protection. I would run their lunch-purchasing errands promptly and with meticulous care not to upset anyone. "Baliol", as the Sixth Form was labeled, could not tolerate ruffled feathers.

It was with this confidence that I dared to loiter among a group of these "sharks", who had stripped down to their swimming trunks, ready for a plunge. All other minnows had escaped. Suddenly, I felt a great big arm on my shoulder, a gentle voice saying "You are due for a swim", and in my imagination, I was already in the water, d-r-o-w-n-i-n-g; it did not matter that I had no swimming trunks. I was soon stripped, hoisted by two giants – one at each end of my anatomy – and thrown into the high tide. After two submersions, emitting brine from nose and mouth, and confident of imminent death, I felt what I imagined to be a shark but which fortuitously turned out to be a hand. When I regained my equilibrium, I realised it was my adult friend of later years, Dr. Oju Mends, Mayor and ardent Masonic brother now deceased, who had retrieved me from the jaws of death. The lasting effect of that experience was my determination to swim, which I did in the company of my equally adventurous classmates, notably Freddie Shears, Alex Short, Josiah Belford and Moses from Wellington Village, all of whom had some previous experience.

Prince of Wales School pupils were always conscious of their connection with British Royalty and tried to pattern their behaviour and activities after the British public school system. Effectively, it was a "public" school without boarding facilities. It was also, in our day, a male secondary school with a British (non-Sierra Leonean) principal.

The sense of responsibility, pride, comradeship, healthy, but fierce competitive spirit wasconsciously instilled into us at every opportunity. We were non-denominational in a society where our competitors often invoked the evangelical foundation of educational institutions as a criticism, but this was easily countered. Ours was the only school not choked with Greek and Theology. Our curriculum was not only liberal but provided the only opportunity for science education with a supporting laboratory. In later years, this initiative paid dividends as our local crop of engineers and doctors began to emerge, virtually all of them men and women being alumni of the Prince of Wales School.

One would have thought that completing a reputable Primary School curriculum and earning a government scholarship for secondary education would guarantee a smooth transition for the school of one's choice. Typical of their generation, my dad had other plans. You could not easily break the family's Methodist tradition and by-pass the Methodist Boys High School (MBHS) for a non-denominational institution like the Prince of Wales School (POW). To complicate my plans, I was made to attempt another MBHS scholarship exam. In what seemed like a conspiracy, I was accepted for Form 2, as against Form 1 in POW, and promised an assured career in the Methodist Ministry. No offer could be more attractive to the family, but for me, I was least interested. For me what was important was the gleaming prospect of the fine day and ceremonial uniforms and every other school equipment – textbooks, exercise books and the special treat of a free daily lunch. I also wanted to be near my friends – Alex Short, Freddie Shears, and Henry Carney who was my infant neighbor. One friend I was going to miss, however, was John Modupeh Taylor-Pearce (aka JTP) who was my daily companion to and from school. We embraced every opportunity for an argument, which neither of us ever lost; this was probably because we were aware of the Confucian wisdom "He who strikes the first blow has lost the argument". It was refreshing to be re-united at faculty level in Fourah Bay College, only to discover that we both remembered the clarion tune with which we whistled to each other. We embraced warmly at his 80th birthday celebration, nine months after mine.

Leaving Ebenezer Amalgamated School had its sentimental trial almost like turning one's back on a devoted nurse. In the intervening years, a constant decline in educational standards may have resulted in the demise of a once famous scholastic foundation stone.

Our teachers at POW were very good in their subjects, patient in their teaching and mercifully, with one or two exceptions, disinclined to use the cane. We were being trained to be self-disciplined young gentlemen. There was, in fact, an official cane in the Principal's office, and every instance of its use was recorded in the punishment book. Lashing was invariably inflicted with the tongue and in such a manner that exposed you to ridicule that could be very lasting. Memorable exponents of such lashing linger in our minds. There was Hugh Clarke a self-proclaimed 'Brumagem' (product of Birmingham) with a distinct accent. During his English classes, he deflated us by recounting his many travels and experiences. We thought some of them may have been exaggerated – e.g. when he told us he had seen white and black swans, Sam Dixon–Fyle wanted to know the length of each ones neck. He moved his hands up and down from one foot to four feet, saying "Like this". Next day, he entered the class and caught Sam repeating the demonstration – words and all! He was thrown out of the class for the next week and we all sympathised with him.

Initiation was, and I suspect, still is an inevitable rite of passage in all boys secondary schools. It can be painful and demeaning to one who is particularly conscious of having graduated into a 'high school'. I discovered and do recommend to all new entrants the successful strategy of appearing to be defenseless, feigning friendship and smiling even after a very gentle brush over the occiput which replaces the vigorous slap from behind. Harsh resistance is tantamount to attempted suicide. In my case, being a diminutive elicited much sympathy and in some cases, patronsing protection. After acclimatisation, it was business as usual – getting to know the routine – and the teachers.

A.T. Thomas made the study of English Literature pleasant and desirable with his singsong diction, while F.B. Harding exuded mathematical precision in all his activities. His steps appeared to be measured to the centimeter per second; his speech precise and unemotional. Even his national nickname "Dyke" was like a mathematical problem defying solution as none of us could discover its meaning or origin.

"Spaddy", our Latin guru, had such a distinctly paterfamilias look in his gait and bearing that we would almost forget that his real name was Mr. Davies. His success as a teacher was so remarkable that all of us at the Cambridge Junior and Senior School Leaving exams, preferred to attack "unseen" translation in which we encountered the passage for the first time.

Sam Forster and C.E. Tuboku-Metzger (later Principal) were real favourites as science teachers, as they gave us the opportunity to experiment with Bunsen burners, pipettes and acids and bases to produce the offensive H_2S gas! Out of the lab, we thoroughly enjoyed the frog-hunting foraging in the field for experimental purposes in Biology. Testing our strength against the vacuum pumps in the physics class was also a favorite experiment for self-assured teenagers, however ineffective the result.

Equally reasonable was Lewis J. Pratt – methodical, neat, unruffled, and Mr. Spilsbury's opposite in the caning game. He taught English without any fuss – and succeeded. Two of the last three featured prominently in my professional career in later years.

No one can forget the legendary A. E. Spilsbury (aka Alfa). The down-to-earth disciplinarian's SM HERO – Saskatchewan, Michigan, Huron, Erie, Rudolph, Ontario put his six great lakes in easy acronym. Always eager to handle the stick and the punishment book, he evinced fear and trembling so that no work was ever neglected.

Our school struck a fine balance between the classroom and recreation; this was readily realised, since ours was probably the only secondary school in Freetown with the playing field adjacent to the classrooms.

The appearance of "Organised Games" on a timetable was sufficient evidence of the importance attached to that activity. Cricket, soccer and athletics were the major activities, but boxing and table tennis later crept in and they were all embraced with sufficient dedication to produce champions at the national level in almost every department.

To recall a few examples: Ola Koroma, my classmate, was easily the nation's fastest bowler, whose ferocity blew away my bat and stumps past the wicket-keeper, thus putting an end to any cricketing dream I was nursing. Desmond Luke, as the high jump champion, not only introduced the western roll but also fine-tuned his skill to become an Oxford blue.

Alex Dunn was our fastest national runner in any race from 100 to 440 yards. On a memorable occasion, he fell as he approached the home stretch, recovered and dusted himself before continuing to win the race in the inter-secondary school sports. We have never been sure whether it was an accident or forgivable showmanship but every Princewalean, and even some rivals, greeted it with raucous acclamation.

Our senior relay team was to other schools as the Jamaican relay team of 2013 was to other national teams – unbeatable.

Even in table tennis, which had very restricted patronage, we were able to produce a Tejan-Cole, who became national champion.

The crowning glory of our sporting achievements was when boxing was introduced as a sport. At our 'Tiny Tots' level, to which I belonged, nobody ever won. Victor Williams (Pendeh),

Josiah Belford (Boys Kobo), Henry Carney and myself always ended our bouts in the ring in a draw; of course, the verbal contest always continued even in the classroom, with each one claiming victory and vowing to be more decisive next time. My constant friend, Ahmed Alami, was a moderating influence.

Deep in our hearts, we did not mind. We preferred to bask in the outstanding exploits of our two heroic classmates, Freddie Shears and Ahmed Alhadi, who were pitted against representatives from the army. These two great heroes not only floored their opponents but Alhadi actually sent his victim through the ropes on to the spectators!

Our rivals sometimes thought we were boastful but perhaps it is difficult to be ecstatic without appearing to be immodest.

The classroom also had its budding wiz kids who were just irritably unbeatable in their chosen fields. There was Moses, Dixon-Fyle, and Tuboku Metzger upholding his uncle's reputation intact and corning out as a successful engineer in later life. English and Latin did engage some of us in fierce but healthy competition. The Literary and Debating Society (L&DS) was in a category of its own, as it engaged pupils from other classes and was consequently more competitive. Full of fun, well supervised by Mr. A.T. Thomas, it turned out to be a training ground for the political hustings. Its annual prize was highly cherished.

I only wish present and future generations of students would engage in similar rivalry with the emphasis on healthy competition in their academic and recreational pursuits. Only then can we honestly and lustily join in the school song that

"When some well-remembered name grows great, we glow with pride to think that in our youthful days, we struggled at his side."

Interestingly, school leaving looms as a long delayed obsession during one's final year but the actual experience is tinged with overtones of melancholy, bordering on sadness. Suddenly, we become more aware of the intersection between transition and transformation. Because of its physical connotation, transition – the movement from one situation to another – is constantly noted, and recorded, leaving experiences that imprint themselves in subtle or blatant ways on the receptive mind.

Unaware of their cumulative impact while absorbing the imprints from life's changing locations and experiences, we suddenly arrive at milestones, crossroads and other temporal and spatial boundaries that compel us to pause, contemplate and recognise our transformation. So it must be, and certainly was, with me, as I floated semi-consciously through the rites of passage. From the helpless infant, denoted by some cultures in the neuter gender, from that physical amoral mass, whose sole purpose was to exhibit the mysterious presence of life in every limb, the evolving self is ultimately confronted with its own metamorphosis and transformation. Halted between the exit door of the playful pupil and the entrance gate to the challenges of adulthood, there is the nagging temptation to exclaim 'Eureka' but without the ecstasy of Euripides. What have we found indeed?

The school is behind us and ahead is the world without end. At that moment, we have only ourselves – a motley band of strips and pieces bound together in some innate cohesion, which proclaims our transformation.

We were now big boys but small men – especially those of us who skipped 6th Form for various reasons. In my case, literary proficiency could not compensate for my weak performance in chemistry – and domestic difficulties complicated the situation. For some people, leaving school also severs what others continue to cherish, as the old school tie. Special anniversaries may sometimes activate links with old friends but the sprout is short lived and fades before it blossoms. Not so, with the thoroughbred Princewaleans, 'Leaving school' does not mean 'Leaving the school'. On the contrary, the strings of tradition and communal fellowship grow even stronger as the days and moments lengthen. Fortunately, the annual prize-giving, sports meeting (at the school grounds) and the thanksgiving service provide opportunities for post-school interaction. To ensure that every past and present pupil could participate in the thanksgiving, the innovation of simultaneous services in church and mosque was instituted. This was vivid evidence of our much-vaunted religious tolerance.

Old Princewaleans President with contemporary friends during annual Thanksgiving Service March

The Old Princewaleans Association has been undulating in fervour during its comparatively short life span, serving with encouraging vigour. I was encouraged by the support we received during my three years of Presidency, when we were able to build a wall around the recreation field. I am sure I benefited from the momentous effort of my predecessor, Dr. Arthur Stewart, who held the Association's meetings in his surgery to save members the tedious late afternoon journey to distant Kingtom in competition with incessant funeral processions.

As I write, the Association is back in excellent health and my fervent prayer and appeal to all past pupils is to sustain its FORWARD movement.

5
A Wider Wilder World

Emerging from the relative security of the classroom, the world beyond appeared fearfully unkind. Fully aware that there were no funds for higher education, I readily accepted the futility of making any such plans. I therefore embarked mentally on a job-hunting assignment without even knowing where to start. Fortunately, a grand uncle, Mr. Kini Thomas, who was still in active employment as the cashier at Elder Dempster Lines office, ordered me to dress up one morning and accompany him to work. On arrival, I was promptly inducted as Cashier's Assistant. Thus began my working life, which spanned six long decades of a variety of challenges and adventure.

Incidentally, it did not matter that employment of under 21 years of age was described as "boy service". In the office, I was Cashier's Assistant but to my admiring and curious friends, I was the Assistant Cashier.

My perceived elevation came to a realistic end when government (the Establishment Secretary) advertised vacancies for recruitment into the civil service and all my family elders decreed in unison that it would be my best option, as it would entitle me to a GOVERNMENT PENSION! It was a decision I was neither able nor wished to over-ride, although at that stage of my late teenage years, an "old age pension" did not feature among my priorities.

Like most young men at 18, I was carefree and loving it. Being recruited as a customs officer opened up vast opportunities to indulge in such tendencies. The glamour of the immaculate uniform with matching tie and cap, and gold coloured stripes to indicate your rank was both a distraction and an attraction. It was also significant that we were not just civil servants but customs officers.

Our special benefits included overtime payments, days on board merchant ships involving foreign cuisine, drinks and a variety of cigarettes, striking acquaintance with various nationalities and in various ways acquiring experience of foreign lands without ever leaving these shores.

A sailor who wanted to go ashore would sell his expensive watch cheaply for local currency but we did not have money to throw away, so the bargaining was tight.

At Government Wharf, which was our outdoor posting, perhaps the most interesting feature was the variety of characters we had to encounter. The customs officers were generally in charge and ensured that everyone realised and accepted it. In order to dent our credibility, someone would hide a small cargo item (watch, cigarette case or lighter) into one's raincoat pocket and alert the security guards at the gate. My mentor, Sydney Konigbabe Warne, therefore gave me as one of his first commandments, to search myself thoroughly before departure. He was a character to be remembered. Although only a couple of years ahead in the job, the way he strutted, you would think he was a Collector of Customs. Actually, he was just a jovial fellow with whom I shared a lot of fun, especially when we were examining the rubbish bins to remove the stolen items on which the garbage was piled. This meticulous care was reflected in his later assignments as a judge and the first Chairman of the Political Parties Registration Commission.

Another interesting associate in the job was Ola Thomas, the elder brother of Professor Kosonike Koso-Thomas. He was in charge of the correspondence branch, to which I was posted for experience. As an elderly brother, he tried to teach me touch typing; was frustrated by my lack of progress but succeeded in making me fairly proficient with my two point-men. This association became a family friendship that lasted throughout his lifetime and a memory I shall cherish throughout mine.

Ola and I formed a mini consultancy – active though not very lucrative. All customs documents processed at the port were cross-checked at the office and queries issued to the offending officers. We would examine the queries, interview the defaulters, draft and type out the replies for a modest fee when the outdoor officers collected their overtime – a benefit not accessible to office staff. It was all part of the department's culture and accepted in good humour.

As we advertised ourselves in exquisitely tailored uniforms with sober matching ties, few admirers could imagine the degree of adventure we sometimes encountered. One of my incidents was over the serving of breakfast on board an American cargo ship. Our meals were compulsory when on duty, and normally served for the crew and us together. On one occasion, the boarding launch arrived late and the breakfast service had been cleared. They were quite reluctant about laying out again for me alone – at a time when my hollow bowels were being tempted by the irresistible aroma of the ships galley (kitchen). Being desperately hungry, having missed a regular diet of leftover (or cold) rice, I flexed my muscles a bit, whereupon they laid out a gladiators banquet for this tiny fellow, warning me that if I did not finish it, they would throw me overboard and set sail. I was gullible enough to be a bit frightened. I explained that they had quenched my thirst and appetite with fright and this pleased them tremendously. They surrounded me, laughed their sides out and let me gorge myself with portions that were only a mouthful for the smallest of them. We lived happily ever after.

Other experiences were hair-raising. The ships were always berthed far from the jetty so that we had long rides in a launch to reach them. After a while, we got used to the rocking over the billows, feeling like fishermen in training. The real ordeal, however, was climbing into the ship by ascending the 'jacob's ladder' slung over the vessel's side. In calm weather, it was demanding enough, but using the tumultuous heaving of a puny launch as a foothold to grasp an equally elusive ladder on the slippery side of an unsteady ship looked suicidal. The climax of my 'tidewaiting' adventure came near to success at suicide!

On a fiercely stormy, night at the height of the rainy season, I was posted to board a ship anchored far from the jetty as there were no berthing facilities in those days. Armed with my umbrella, official raincoat and Wellington boots, I boarded the launch on what was itself a perilous journey through wind, pouring rain and billowing waves. On arrival at the ship, there was, mercifully, no jacob's ladder. The gangway had been lowered, inviting us to a courteous walk up the stairs. However, between the unsteady edge of the heaving launch and wet, slippery gangway, the jaws of death lurked in silent but ominous invitation beneath the waves. Attempting an adventurous leap across the gap between ship and launch, and with open umbrella in one hand, the launch moved, left my back foot suspended while the other was in flight. As my wellingtons began to sink, I was fortunate to grab the chain supporting the gangway, while an army of horrified observers heaved me to safety on the ships plank as I bid farewell to my umbrella. It took a good few tots of cognac to restore my equilibrium.

Work in the office was less exciting but had its memorable aspects. There was no death experience or ecstatic humour as the

35

prevailing atmosphere was heavy from the presence of stolid unsmiling senior officials whose lack of official humour was a legacy of the British colonial reserve. In that tradition, any show of familiarity or friendliness from seniors is an invitation to indiscipline.

Good or bad weather, lack of transport fare or some domestic calamity was never sufficient excuse for a few minutes lateness. Every such infraction was occasion for a written query to be answered (also in writing) within 24 hours. As an occasional transgressor, I developed a catalogue of excuses that could not be faulted, but this only alienated me further, as I was also branded "unofficial lawyer" for my colleagues in the outdoor branch. I did not mind this label as it brought in lawful supplementary income for me and my friend, Ola Thomas.

From our youngish point of view, those older folk were so mechanical that they seemed sensitively inhuman. During the general strike of 1954, whilst police bullets and teargas were polluting the air, they insisted that we should all report for duty to demonstrate that we were not also on strike. Finding our way to work at the quay situated at the extreme east end of town was challenging enough when about 90 percent of officers were resident in the Central and West wards. Then came the fatal day when the strikers decided to dislodge and involve us. Scaling the hills and bush paths surrounding Freetown, jolted by the staccato of sporadic gunshots, is still a living memory.

I cannot conclude a Customs Department narrative without recalling the wonderful time we had with the Kroo boys. These were the tally clerks and deck hands coming ashore after a tour of duty on board cargo vessels. Their tales just fell short of Drake's reports of 'men with dog's faces or heads beneath their shoulders'.

They delighted us with gifts of yams, cigarette cases and lighters, but an unforgettable classic was the following conversation:

> "What's your name"?
> "T.K. Browne"
> "What's the T for?"
> "Alfred"
> "What's the K for?"
> "That be grandmother name!"

Fortuitously, Divine Providence had ordained that government scholarships would be awarded the year following the strike for qualified officers to pursue degrees at Fourah Bay College, presumably in preparation for the post-independence era.

For me, it was, as much a challenge and an honour. On my first appearance at an international conference, the average age and appearance of my peers made me feel almost like an overgrown teenager. Thereupon, I decided to disguise myself with a beard. For several years, as I was armed with a Cuban cigar in a briar holder and decorated with an unfamiliar beard, even my contemporaries had difficulty recognising me.

Having been reared on such a variety of experiences in my first full-time job, I had to leave a lot of baggage behind on my transition to the next stage of my life.

6
Road to Athens (FBC)

Separation from the world of work for a prematurely married young man was a traumatic prospect, but Divine Providence in the guise of ministerial leaders like Albert Margai, HEB John and Barthes Wilson had ordained that serving officers on study leave should receive their salaries for their domestic obligations and student allowance for their college expenses. This for me was an outcome of relief.

Prior to our admission, the campus had not been one of my consuming interests. As I recall, we invariably passed through as a group in the company of our friend and classmate, Hudson Ashwoode, to test the variety of fruit in his father's farm even before they were certified ready for the market. Those were eating days – and boys ate voraciously! This time there was a hesitant, almost timid procession to campus. Emotions fluctuated from the uncertainty of the unknown to the determination of scaling and overcoming new heights.

The road to Athens was paved with uneven pebbles of certainty, permitting only cautious steps, but the beckoning horizon offered reassuring rewards – the prospect of a profession with a Durham University degree, which is highly rated universally. As I discovered later, the COD Universities in England referred to Cambridge, Oxford and Durham.

As we realised when we all converged at college, the Customs Department probably released the largest contingent of officers, and they proved themselves worthy of the opportunity. When they were re-deployed later in the service, Freddie Harleston, the only one who returned to the Customs, retired as Comptroller; Bob King was Financial Secretary and C. D. Williams, as Permanent Secretary of Trade and Industry, virtually controlled the country's economy. When I joined them at the then relatively young age of 38 as Permanent Secretary of the Foreign Affairs Ministry, our contingent was complete. Being one of the three youngest Permanent Secretaries in the service was considered a distinction-- and so it probably was for Prince Taylor–Lewis, my other colleague who soared to the World Bank later; as well as Ahmad Tejan Kabbah, who excelled as a Director at the United Nations, followed by two terms as President of the land that we love, our Sierra Leone.

For us, mature greenhorns, the initial problem was one of assimilation into a group fresh from the classroom. Being relatively young myself and of minimal stature, my assimilation was quite easy. To my surprise also, keeping constantly in mind the future of my newly created family, the change of lifestyle from the happy-go-lucky mini socialite of a customs officer to the rigorous regime of an ambitious budding academic was virtually flawless.

Student days were a real delight. Exposure to academia was a process of refinement. It raised the student of average means and limited exposure to a new modus vivendi, of which Fourah Bay College was among the most elegant providers on the continent and beyond. Students in the Sub-region were as eager to come here, as they are to proceed to Europe, America and further afield nowadays.

Probably because the numbers were manageable, the organisation was easier. Every student had a personal tutor who acted as a perpetual mentor and provided audience through the social and academic labyrinth of a residential college. Tutorials provided an avenue for enriching interaction with faculty. Reviewing topics and discussing presentations were only the regular part of the programme, and being treated to tea, biscuits and scones were refining experiences.

Since Durham was the mother University of Fourah Bay College in those days, the strict residential aura of the mother institution was virtually replicated on Mount Aureol as I discovered later.

Both students and lecturers attended lectures in their academic gowns; lunch and dinner were served in the dining hall at specified and respected hours; however, whereas the former was informal, dinner was strictly formal in terms of academic garb. The High Table was always in attendance, invariably headed by the Warden of Students and on selected occasions by the Principal himself. Formal prayers were offered before service and the latter was orderly and rotational. The hour after dinner would be spent in the canteen buying soft drinks and other refreshments or snacks, and in the Student Common Room playing cards, scrabble, crossword puzzles and other games. Finally, the library ended the average day. In that atmosphere, even the most rustic student could not resist the culture of academic refinement.

Beyond the lecture hall and the formal structures, the students engaged themselves in clubs specific to their academic interests, of which Historical Society, Drama Club, Rhetoric Society and Journalistic Enterprise, with the Aureol Spectator and Aureol Mirror as only two outstanding examples. At a more social level, private clubs, male or female, with membership by invitation and a lecturer or two as patrons, set standards of behaviour for aspiring members.

There was much healthy rivalry among the social clubs, each striving to be the most attractive in terms of good behaviour, providing the most able student leaders, academic successes and generally being the most desirable choice by potential members.

The Tea Club was where I met close friends, including Dennis Woode, Kweku Deigh, who later became Student Representative or Head of the Student Representatives Council, Ransford Roy Macauley and Alusine Deen, who became Ambassador to China. Many of us came to College from the world of work, which gave the Tea Club a special air of maturity. Another peculiarity of our club was the selection of one lady on campus for membership. Within the club, she henceforth became known as "Mr." Our choice was Gloria Ashwoode--very pleasant, sociable and apparently unattached or very discreetly so. Intuitively, without any research, our selected Faculty member turned out to be the lecturer, Eldred Durosimi Jones, only for us to discover later, to our delight, that he had been a member of the original Tea Club at Mabang, where the college spent some of its earlier years. On campus, the Club's socio-intellectual character was unique. Examples of this were the organisation of the first student rag parade to celebrate Ghana's independence and a public debate on campus and later on radio. The argument was about which should precede the other – Political or Economic Independence.

The most significant feature of that debate was the marriage of town and gown in which Siaka Stevens and I were pitted against Albert Margai and Kweku Deigh over the radio.

My FBC experience really prepared me for life at University College Durham, where I soon won the Presidency of Durham Colleges United Nations Student Association, (UNSA) and was also fortunate to lead the University Debating Team to various Universities in England, Scotland and Ireland, losing only once on a return visit to Ireland. It was probably in compensation that I was awarded the Robson Shield as best debater of the year and elevated to the exclusive Chair of President of the Durham's Union Society. I also learned that the honorary membership, which the Historical Society of Trinity College, Dublin conferred on me, was a rare acquisition.

If I sound nostalgic about Fourah Bay College of our day, it is because there was much to be nostalgic about. The mature students among us were looking forward to improvements in our economic and social status after College and because of our work experience, our work ethic was probably more organised and orderly. Thus, we were seen as role models while on our part, every effort was made to integrate smoothly.

Fourah Bay College of the 1950s included among its student body post-graduate, undergraduate diploma and certificate teachers. Science was then an infant faculty gaining ground speedily. In this milieu, academic and social interaction was fluid and widespread to the benefit of all concerned.

Integrity among students was maintained at the highest level because no one would risk jeopardising his/her dignity. Dignity had to be manifested not only in comportment but also in one's academic studies. Everybody knew all the results by heart. In addition, while a reference was a calamity, failure was a catastrophe.

In spite of the mix, numbers were small and manageable so that any infraction or deviant behavior soon became a scandal and labelled the culprit an outcast.

In case I have painted a picture that makes us look like youthful robots, let me fray the edges a bit.

Ms. Dolphin, a very kind and elderly spinster, was very vigilant as Warden of Women Students and would religiously visit the female hostels at unspecified hours to ensure that decorum was being observed and that male students did not overstay their visiting hours, which ended by twilight. After dinner, of course, there was ample opportunity for predators to smile and talk their way into the welcoming hearts of willing young school leavers, who soon became regular partners at the frequent ballroom sessions.

We had other gimmicks too. Dennis Woode was my regular mate with whom I studied and shared an only cigarette when things were rough. By sheer coincidence, we were also the only students with motorbikes. This made us very popular with students whom we pillioned to town in relays. On the contrary, we were regularly hovering on the wrong side of Rev. Solomon Caulker (aka Solo), the Warden of men students, as his residence was on the brow of the steepest hill approaching the campus. At that point, his peaceful sleep was very vulnerable to the roaring of two motor bikes. One night we decided to use only one bike and on arriving at reasonable distance from his Wardenship's residence, we tried to push the vehicle uphill – after a night out! The effort was promptly abandoned, and the bike was soon roaring uphill. Next morning, with a twinkle in both eyes, our doyen warned that "gating" would come into full force. This would mean confinement to campus for a specified period. Fortunately, we were his favorite Philosophy students and being mature students, we were treated with kid gloves.

It was the joint team of "Solo" and Rev. Fergusson, who endeared Dennis and me to Philosophy. "Fergo" had a double 1st class in both Oxford and Cambridge and when Durham reported that I had top marks in the University's Colleges in 1st year Philosophy, he threw off his clerical reserve and actually hugged me. "Solo B" took over and convinced me to accept the "offer" of an Honours course in Durham, although deep down I preferred English Language and Literature. It is a sad reflection that at the point of my Durham graduation, Rev. Caulker's plane on the way home crashed into the sea off Dakar. Requiescat in Pace.

Our younger colleagues from school may have been only so in age and experience but they were very spirited and unyielding in argument. For those of us who were predominantly from boys' schools and the workplace, it was revealing and refreshing to encounter the lively intelligence of young female adults. Little wonder that virtually all of our colleagues in the class rose to some prominence – Florence Dillsworth as Mayor, Clarice Coker, Grace Nelson-Williams and Gloria Ashwoode as outstanding educationists, Ajayi Coomber as international linguistics lecturer, Dennis Woode as Deputy Establishment Secretary and George Anthony (my constant rival in English and Latin) a distinguished historian. The list goes on...

Against this background and bearing in mind the impact of the civil servants who benefited and returned to assist Sierra Leone to and through independence, we owe a debt of deep gratitude to our pre-independence leaders for their foresight.

7
Durham Unveiled

Leaving our very own Athens, an outreach of Durham, one felt justified in assuming that nothing would change except the climate and more precise use of the language. The climatic difference was an unforgettable experience, which will be illustrated by few incidents. As for the language, one had to be fluent in two 'dialects': one on campus and the other for the city to facilitate assimilation into the city. There was a clear linguistic distinction between the campus folk and the local "Geordies."

In the end, the entire trip to Durham and back was a compendium of transformatory experiences. Having completed my maiden flight to Accra for the World University Service (WUS) meeting, I expected no surprises en route to London. My initiation into a new lifestyle took place at Dakar airport where we were served breakfast after spending the night. After devouring a goodly portion of a French roll and three large croissants, I was offered water, which turned out to be a sizable portion of "Perrier." Trouble erupted when I was presented a bill for the Perrier. For a student in transit, breakfast, including water, was supposed to be free. In any case, this fellow had no currency, local or foreign as I had been dispatched in penury, expecting to find El Dorado at the other end. I made my Franglais deliberately unintelligible, sheepishly absorbed the managers' explanation that in francophone culture, Perrier was served for water and chargeable. My plight was accepted, however, with a kindly admonition to be guided in future. I cannot recall spending another day or night at Dakar airport.

The rest of the trip was uneventful, but on arrival in London, I dreamt of the stereotype images of British life – eggs, muffins, mustard, Yorkshire pudding, roast beef and the inevitable cup of fine tea; of course, there would be cricket, the pub, the odd concert and visits to monuments and other places of interest. However, the reality of my first priority – shopping for warm clothing-- soon dawned on me.

On arrival in the city, I was soon jolted back to the reality of Sierra Leone when my old friend and comrade–in–arms at the Customs, Ola Thomas, appeared at the British Council and whisked me off to join the Sierra Leone conclave at his residence at 8 Wolfington Road, West Norwood. This homely abode became my travellers rest and domestic base throughout my sojourn in the UK and subsequent visits. Here were assembled an array of resident and itinerant students, including some couples. I recall Kosonike Koso-Thomas, the younger brother of Ola; Rodney Fergusson-Williams; Daniel Chaytor, who became Koso's brother-in-law whilst a student; Gilpin; Jonah; the Johnston couple; Ola's spouse, Louisa, and her two brothers – the Coles. It was such a lively bunch that during college breaks, we felt like being on holiday back home. Of special interest was the easy availability of home cooking.

Playing WHOT and Scrabble whilst discussing Cold War and African liberation issues and viewing Koso's latest paintings kept us active and animated. With hilarious Krio proverb competitions and the weddings during vacations, there was never a dull moment. Of course, it was easy to secure decent vacation jobs in London at reputable elite institutions like the banks, BBC, and Lancôme Salon. All you needed was a fitting blazer, immaculate shirt collar with your college tie and an impressive mastery of BBC elocution when addressing the young ladies at Brooke Street Employment Bureau. Too bad for our new generation of African students, as there are too many applicants these days and the novelty of that approach has probably worn off.

You can see from all this that 8 Wolfington Road remains a treasured memory for our generation of students, many of whom I fondly recall, especially those who have passed away.

After the chequered trip to Durham, my arrival proved to be a real climax. The entrance to the city was by a bridge, wide enough to admit only one car at a time. This was strategically located within a curve so that drivers approaching from either side would be unaware of each other until they met at the bridge with neither in a position to reverse or give way. To obviate this impasse, a television control station was cited in the city controlling traffic lights at the bridge. Uniquely, this was the only traffic light in all England controlled by television. Pictures of Durham Castle had only partially revealed its noble dominance of the city around it. In reality, it was a majestic presence. Standing at the gate to the porter's lodge brought back visions of a world that was suddenly both old and new; old because it represented centuries of historic conflict with the Norsemen, episodes of rugged gentility, wine and wassail. For me, however, it was a new adventure into an unfolding ethos, with none of my old campus comrades, no family to visit at weekends, and no escape to the City Hotel for Saturday lunchtime encounters with the young crop of politicians who engaged us in student reflection while wetting our whistles.

The porter's welcome was kindly but measured and as I signed in, the cold air seemed to emerge from the stonewalls and enveloped me. I was actually shivering all the way to the 2nd floor, where a door was opened and I was ushered into a room that became my dorm until my wife arrived. Left alone in the room, it transformed itself into an icebox closing in on me.

Thus began my first adventure in College on the night of my arrival. It was now late September, and the regulations did not permit the central heating to be turned on before 1 October. Spurred by some fast but misguided insight, I tucked the reading lamp between the sheets and hurried off for a drink and a bite at the Three Tuns–the local pub, which was prominently advertised on my way in. Fortified and sweating from the addition of a brisk walk, I entered my room and was nearly blinded by the bulb, which had burnt its way through the sheets and was staring at me accusingly. Too tired to react, I ducked under what was left of the sheets and dreamt of a hot sunny afternoon at Lumley Beach, which was until then the tourists' paradise in West Africa.

I woke up confronted by the daunting prospect of reporting my misadventure to my porter's lodge. Fortuitously, the staff were a jovial bunch who were laughing their heads off whilst consoling me. They even provided me with a paraffin heater until the heating was turned on.

Recovering my equilibrium, I began to absorb the breath taking reality of Durham Castle as an iconic symbol. It was part of a trilogy consisting of the Castle, the Cathedral and the Durham Union Society, linked in serene communion by the tranquil beauty of Palace Green. Such serenity was, of course, disturbed, but only slightly when folks like us – in statu pupilari – interposed ourselves upon this idyllic reality. On balance, one absorbed what we neither could nor would destroy. Durham thus infiltrated and became an enduring element in the transformation of its alumni.

Durham Castle and, indeed, the ancient city were elevated to their most celestial realm at daybreak on Sunday morning when Music from the Organ Loft infiltrated the waking consciousness in melodious chiming bells mixed with such keyboard dexterity that one's spirit was transported to the highest realms. On my first Sunday morning, the poetic lines that infiltrated my thoughts included

"Music that gentler on the spirit lies than tired eyelids upon tired eyes" or
"Music that softer on the spirit falls like petals from blown roses on the grass"
Then followed Milton's majestic blast

47

"From harmony, from Heavenly Harmony this universal frame began"

Inspired, I crawled out of bed, unmindful of the chill outside, fortified myself with an extra layer of underclothes, and with very clear direction from the porter's lodge, I found my way to the local Methodist Church to worship in my own familiar tradition. Thus began an unforgettably happy involvement in the life of Durham city.

Since students had not returned to the campus, the presence of two Africans in the church was conspicuous. The other was Edna Konotey-Ahulu, a young Ghanaian student reading music. She was being mentored in Durham by the church organist, Bill Harrison, and his wife, Nellie. After service, they invited me to lunch at their residence at "Ainsdale, 14 Long Acres, Durham", which turned out to be my home away from campus until my wife arrived and took over. Even after we moved into rented digs, Ainsdale remained our home.

I am fairly certain there was never a kindlier couple in all of Durham. They were a portly, loving, and loveable couple, presumably in their mid-50s. Bill was an official in the newspaper business in Gateshead, and left very early to catch the train. He was a typical Geordie, the local collective name for North-easterners. They are forthright, down-to-earth and very loyal to any cause they embrace. We benefited from this particular trait. Being childless, they enrolled us as their siblings by natural selection. Bill was always with Edna, especially at the piano, and as a one–time chorister, I would lead the singsong when she was not flexing her fingers on Arabesque or the Moonlight Sonata.

Nellie spoilt me--- what with laundry, ironing, darning, and socks replacement, regular meals, an electric blanket warming my bed while I sipped my nightcap, birthday camera and accessories. My faith tells me they must have a place in Heaven. I only hope we can recognise each other and reunite if I secure a place there.

Bill and Nellie Harrison – my mentors in Durham

I thoroughly enjoyed the two worlds of my Durham experience – the cloistered shades of Cathedral and Castle, with all their organised formality, left an indelible imprint of the COD culture in its inmates, while the expansive generosity and rugged friendliness of the coal mining population challenged the lure of the homestead at West Norwood and Brook Street Bureau earnings that drew me from my idyllic location.

The collegiate life was a virtual replica of the Fourah Bay College (FBC) routine. The hours for lectures, recreation, dining hall, and extra-curricular activities were defined and rigid. There was also much room for a variety of activities--a fact reminiscent of our Athens. Actually, the advantage in this area was in FBC's favour, probably reflecting the cultural difference between English reserve and African hyperactivity.

Building on my experience as a Secretary-General of the United Nations Students Association (UNSA) and World University Service (WUS) at FBC, I joined both and to my pleasant surprise was eventually elected President of Durham Colleges UNSA. In this capacity, I made my first trip to continental Europe as the representative at an international students' conference and I could not help recalling how a Nigerian was part of our FBC delegation to WUS at Legon, Accra.

Encouraged by the assimilation, I turned to sports and games embracing table tennis and soccer for a start, but soon discovered the agony of being hard hit by a fast moving football on a bleak autumn evening. It was farewell to soccer dreams. Table tennis was indoors, required more concentration and success or failure was dependent on just yourself. Somehow, I was recruited into the College team, which meant missing our dinners when playing matches out of campus, but there was the compensating thrill of fish and chips in a newspaper cone. One felt really integrated into the culture.

Extra-curricular activities were really absorbing, especially when I became involved in the debating activities of the Durham Union Society. I came to realise that a Union Society is a cardinal institution in every reputable University in the British Isles. Oxford and Cambridge were pre-eminent, but Durham, Edinburgh, Glasgow, Dublin, and London were also in the premier league. My first invitation was to lead a proposition with which I in fact disagreed. The subject was:

> That whilst this House regrets the sentiment, it approves the proposition
> "Wogs begin at Calais"

For my readers' benefit, WOG is an abbreviation for Western Oriental Gentlemen. Against all expectation, including mine, the proposition won handsomely and my debating reputation rocketed sky-high. Based on that initial performance, I was elected to the

Executive Committee, appointed leader of the Union's external debating team and eventually awarded the Robson Shield as the Best Debater of the Year. As team leader, it was my good fortune to enjoy expenses—paid trips to London, Glasgow, Edinburgh and Dublin, as well as hosting Trinity and Edinburgh. We lost only one debate by one vote to the Historical Society in Dublin, which left us square with them. I was consoled by being made Honorary Member of "The Hist." My two fold debating regret was my inability to accept the invitations (I) to the Cambridge Union and (II) to compete for the Observer Mace as both were in conflict with my final year examination term. The climax to all these developments was the Union's gracious and generous gesture in appointing me the first non-English President.

Coleridge, winner of the Robson Shield as best debater of the year, Durham University U. K. 1960

Deferring reference to my academic experience to this point is intended to emphasize that it was the main aim and climax of my presence there. Being presented with the option of a two or three year course, I chose the shorter more intense course to compensate for the three years I had already spent at FBC. It turned out to be a mouthful and probably affected the quality of my degree being below my expectation. However, the letter from the Post-Graduate Department comforted me that I would need only a dissertation, no lectures or exams for a Master's Degree. After submitting my topic, and an evolving conflict with our Education representative overseas, my cumbersome status as a Civil Servant shelved the project. Moreover, my growing interest in international relations, which was emerging as an attractive option with Sierra Leone's independence a few months away, drove my project underground. Mobility within a diplomatic career was all consuming and not conducive to distance education.

On our campus, the academic regime was unrelenting, especially in the disciplines of the Classics, Philosophy, Theology, Languages, and History. Research was rigorously encouraged in these areas while the scientific arm of the University's work – Medicine, Engineering etc. was concentrated at Newcastle upon–Tyne.

Upon reflection, the University seemed to have a peculiar preference for compartmentalisation. There were no coed colleges. Hatfield, St. Mary's, St. Aidan's, St. John's and the Castle were all gender specific, although the Castlemen, occupying tow medieval castles six miles apart, often assumed an air of feebly contestable superiority. What with a porter's lodge, the coal shoot for illicit nocturnal access to our rooms, and the Great Hall where the Queen and Prince Philip had lunch with Durham's Nobility (including your Union President!)

Of our lecturers, Dr. Von Leyden appeared the most distinguished; unfortunately he reminded me of the traditional unflattering view of Africans held by earlier German philosophers when he reflected on the African preference for Law and was intrigued by my choice of a career in Philosophy.

Our tutorials were not as homely as at FBC, partly because all except one were held in classrooms. There was little interactive effect with our lecturers from these sessions but they brought our small squad of four closer together academically and emotionally. Our Honours Degree class of four was probably the smallest in Durham. Frank Coulthard, Jim Harrison, Shando Lerant (Hungarian) and I were serviced by 4 lecturers in 8 subjects. Our trips to Dr. Von Leyden's home took us along the meandering banks of the River Weir, which was at its most beautiful in mid-winter. It was the season when the river froze solid, inviting the more adventurous students to walk across. Even though we heard stories of the odd accident in previous years of the odd fellow falling between cracks and surviving, we never witnessed any. In fact, for lack of evidence, our philosophical inclination doubted the stories, as recovery from that mass of frozen immersion seemed virtually impossible.

In spite of the earthy mining environment of the county with its rugged image, Durham exuded an atmosphere of friendliness and innocent curiosity. On the bus, curious mothers, abandoning the traditional British reserve, would whisper with a disarming smile "Would you let me touch your hair? It was so fascinating." Once permitted, the sibling would soon be leaning on my shoulder, hair touching of course! I must confess I took the opportunity to exchange compliments, which developed into family friendships with some regular bus travellers. They were always eager to talk about their hobbies—a church fete on Saturdays, support for Newcastle football club, watching county cricket and migrating to Gateshead and Newcastle for the seasonal treat of ballroom dancing. After my wife joined me and I moved from the Castle into digs, I was able to enjoy some of these community diversions.

Our landlady, Mrs. Anne Spirlet, who had divorced her foreign husband, kept us really busy while her teenage children were left to their own devices. With Olivia's permission, while awaiting the fourth of our six daughters, Anne Spirlet recruited me as her ballroom dancing partner, reminding me very vividly of one's Fourah Bay experience.

At the other end of the spectrum was the elegant serenity of Durham. The disciplined respect for the lecture timetable included strict punctuality, duration of lectures and assignment presentation. The dining hall was similarly regulated—academicals, punctuality, prayers and the High Table invariably filled by the Master and Faculty.

Union Society nights were equally punctilious. Dress was strictly formal for the debaters, the president, and any special guest invited to the preceding Dinner at the Three Tuns—the only classy tavern in town. The timing was always precise—an obvious significant improvement on my West African experience. Similarly, as the debaters' correspondent, my report submission was just as precise. It is hoped that those of our students who read these lines will be sufficiently impressed to follow the Durham example.

Apart from the chiming bells on Sunday mornings, which prepared me for attendance at the Methodist Church, I must appear to have ignored Durham Cathedral. It was in fact among my indelible memories. The architecture complementing the Castle, the celestial harmony of its choral repertoire and its imposing majesty are unforgettable.

Sanctifying the imposing Castle with its celestial serenity, it compelled memories of the moat, the mural and the historic battles to fade into significance. One last recollection of the Castle is its aesthetic appearance in my student camera, reflected so faithfully in the undisturbed calm of the summer surface of the River Weir that even I, the photographer, had difficulty deciding which way was original as distinct from the reflection.

Before leaving Durham finally, two of the most outstanding events of my sojourn deserve special mention.

On 30 May 1960, the day I started my final exams, we welcomed the new arrival, our fourth baby, Helen, who grew up to be amongst the loveliest and most affectionate of my daughters.

It was also during these last days that I was invited as President of the Union to join the welcoming party for Her Majesty Queen Elizabeth II and H.R.H. Prince Philip on their visit to the University. After our lunch in the Castle, I chatted with both of them, shook hands like any student in that privileged position and ended my day on cloud nine.

8
Australia and Back

Leaving Durham in December 1960, I was now qualified for a senior service position. Alternative prospects loomed with varying degrees of clarity but the ultimate decision for a civil servant always comes from the Administration. Personally, I was divided between an academic and a diplomatic career. The final decision was dictated by circumstances, as we were due for independence in a few months.

Tragically, my Philosophy mentor, Solomon B. Caulker, died in a plane crash off the Dakar coast: he was returning home from leave just as I was graduating. I would have still pursued the academic option after a postgraduate degree for which the University only required me to submit a dissertation with no course work. In familiar style, the civil service ordained that I should return immediately for a posting to the provinces. My enquiries about the Foreign Service were summarily eclipsed with the reply that there were no vacancies for recruits. This surprised me at a time when the embryo of the service was far from the hatching stage.

With resignation, and by Divine Providence, the Australian Government offered a Diplomatic Training Scholarship with duration extended from 3 months to 1 year. I may have been the only applicant since I received acceptance and instructions within a week, instructing me to report in Sydney within 14 days. In the midst of packing, while my wife was still in London expecting another baby, my emotion wavered through elation, expectation, and hesitation.

Of course, I was elated at my automatic selection without even the formality of an interview; expectation was high but rather vague, as Australia was then rather distant from West Africa in time and space as well as in our imagination. It was at the end of the world, and not easily accessible to us. Growing in my emotions, however, was the much-vaunted White Australia policy. Stories of maltreatment of the Aborigines were literally translated into similar treatment of all non-whites with Africans top of the list.

This anxiety was put to rest after discussion with Donald George, the beneficiary of the previous year's three-month course. It turned out that while the issue of entry and residential visas to non-whites was very restricted, those admitted received right royal treatment. I had foretaste for such treatment as a first class passenger from Freetown to Sydney, spending most of those hours on board an Australian Quantas flight.

Australia, with more open spaces, was different from the UK. Australians were a free and less reserved people, down-to-earth in their relationships, frank almost to a fault and very outdoor and sport oriented. We were three trainees, the other two being from South Korea and Malaysia. Through the latter, I was able to spend three days in transit in Kuala Lumpur sampling spicy mutton-based delicacies and the lavish spread of their sprawling hotel apartments. The South Korean experience came later during an official Ministerial delegation with Foreign Minister Francis Minah to Seoul. This visit has lasted most in my memory, as it was my last official trip as a member of the Foreign Ministry.

Leaving England in December when fingers in gloves were freezing to arrive three months later in Sydney where it would be even colder soon was not an exotic expectation but the prospect of a 36-hour experience as the prepaid guest of a first class intercontinental airline was enough to suspend my initial anxiety. With the vision of my chosen career beckoning over the horizon, excitement dominated the other emotions… Rome, Alaska, Singapore, Manilla, Biak – a really exotic route, which I noted to be explored in later years on active service. For the moment, we were savouring the Mediterranean, The Alps, the emerald sea below where visible and azure canopy above; a kaleidoscope of merging colours at sunrise and sunset as we pursued the sun in its apparent westward flight.

The arrival was as friendly and informal as only Australians can make it. There was I, expecting a formal British "Welcome Mr. Coleridge-Taylor" accompanied by a measured handshake.

In its place, I received a very hearty handclasp, a warm and vigorous shake with a real Aussie drawl, which sounded like "Mr. Calry-Taylor", after which we reduced it all into first names. Discovering later that I was only one of three non-Australians on the programme made me feel almost like an alien, since I was the only one from outside Australasia. Lee was from Seoul, South Korea and Talala from Malaysia. As our interaction progressed, I realised what a great opportunity it offered not only to learn about distant, foreign cultures but also to discuss our individual and collective vision of our decolonised nations. The training experience was further complicated but eventually enriched by being merged with the entire corps of Australian recruits.

Returning to the classroom after the rigours of Durham was not an inviting prospect, but full time final year classes in International Relations and Economics proved indispensable in grooming a philosopher for a diplomatic career.

Out of the classroom and the office desk, the programme provided a vivid and comprehensive exposure to this Southern continent, its life and work, and most impressively, to the character of its people.

After the rather withdrawn and hesitant interaction typical of the average Briton, adjustment to the expansive Aussi required some attitudinal behavioral realignment. Being a diplomat in training also required certain restraints in a society where strictly diplomatic observance was ignored or ridiculed. The average Australian's character opens wide into multidimensional panorama upon contact, no previews, and no shorts. No one, for instance, says "King's Cross" when referring to the Geo-Cultural Centre of Sydney, the nation's capital. It is recognised and known only as "King's Bloody Cross." In fact, a gentle inoffensive swearword punctuates every sentence to make it palatable and intelligible to indigene and visitor alike. Swearing at a companion was an acknowledged act of friendly acceptance. Failing to return it, on the other hand, was unfriendly and snobbish.

The beauty of Australia was displayed by its variety-- reflected in its climate, the changing features in its landscape, extreme conditions, and its various peoples and cultures.

Its southern tip revealed the snowy mountains, which we visited on a training session only for the wheels of the bus to be buried for days in frozen ice. Up in the Northern territories where the lush greenery and tropical temperature embraced me with familiar warmth, the locals were even more effusive. Recognising me as a son of the tropics, offers of tropical fruit came in relays – pineapple, paw paw, coconut, guava – ripened by the sun and sweetened further by the warmth of their smiles and laughter.

We were so extensively exposed because, as we soon discovered, there was no special training programme for foreign diplomats. Effectively, we would end up as trained Australian diplomats with insights into the intricacies of Commonwealth and 'Western' diplomacy. Probably, the intention was to cultivate in us a sympathetic attitude toward their ideology and perceptions in a world that was still strongly bi polar. The advantage to us was that when we graduated into non-aligned movement, our perception of the gulf separating the opposing sides was much clearer and more informed.

Another advantage was that the Australian experience provided us with a model for designing a full training course for our own or other diplomats as opposed to 3-month short-term programmes. The downside was that in order to operate effectively in our own context, we would have tuned it to suit our own geo-political environment. African diplomacy was after all in its infancy and just developing in both content and style. In later years, it was not enough to be just a West African diplomat. If you could be both an international and African diplomatist simultaneously, operating in context, as appropriate, you had an extra notch to your belt.

Being a leading member of the South East Asia Treaty Organization (SEATO) with unmistakable sympathies toward the North Atlantic Treaty Organization (NATO) through its umbilical British links conferred on Australia distinct geo-political and strategic advantages. These advantages became obvious as we discussed spheres of influence in the Final Year Political Science class at the Australian National University, where we were enrolled. This course, by exposing various types of statecraft--autocratic, democratic, free and centralised economies--provided us with ammunition to face the variety of presentations and choices floating in international diplomacy. There was no truer mix of these than at the United Nations.

We were not confined to classrooms. The practical aspect was equally alive. Visits to every State gave us insights at first hand into the geography, history, and economic and cultural diversity of this vast sub-continent and soon endeared it to us.

Visits to various Commonwealth High Commissions and Embassies provided a foretaste of the life ahead while affording us the chance to observe variations in practical matters like internal consultations and communication flow, security and even assignments. Even our entertainment was largely organised, although we cautiously stepped out of line when convenient.

Officially, we would dine rotationally at the homes of middle level diplomats, sampling exotic cuisine and playing croquet on the lawn at weekends, leaving room for sports and games, of course, as this was an essential ingredient on any Australian social menu.

A memorable development of our stay was the establishment of a social group labelled the "Refugees Club". It was conceived and operated as a welcome weekend respite for foreign trainees in the Australian working week tradition. Friday evening in the Australian workmen's calendar was probably the justification for the popular expression "TGIF" (Thank God It's Friday). The working week ended at 5pm on that day but was inevitably followed by a mass gathering at every available pub within the shortest possible time. Sitting in groups of 10-12, everyone was obliged to order a round (aka "a shout") to be consumed before the tables were cleared as the pubs were obliged to stop serving alcohol by 7pm. The joke went around that the easiest way to attempt suicide was to cross the road between 7 and 8pm on a Friday!

To obviate this danger, our resourceful liaison officer decided that we should have a Friday luncheon, to which we invited middle level diplomats---at least we could observe and learn from them conveniently; we labeled it "prayers" initially but later christened it "Refugees Club."

To our surprise and pleasure, the club grew in size and status to include acting Heads of Missions (Acting High Commissioners and Charge d'affaires) by the time we were returning home.

Three years later in 1964, while serving the Sierra Leone Mission to the UN in the Committee on Decolonisation, I was selected by the UN Secretariat to be part of a mission to observe the Decolonisation process in Papua, New Guinea under Australia's administration.

This meant stopping over in Australia once more, and to my pleasant surprise, I was met by my training liaison officer, Ian Hamilton, who chaperoned me to a meeting of the Refugee lunch. It had grown beyond our wildest dreams and now included Ambassadors, NGO heads and UN officials. When introduced as one of its founders, I was virtually speechless. Fortunately, my UN interaction facilitated my composure. On my third visit to

Australia, en route to New Zealand, I was unable to visit but I hope it is still thriving.

Australians work hard and play even harder. From the "new Austrians", mainly from Eastern Europe (Poland, Czechoslovakia etc.) with whom I lived in a hostel, we learnt even more about our host country. We interacted socially, acquired strange tastes like oyzo and schlivovitz, and I discovered that through familiarity, we helped them to overcome prejudices, which sometimes distinguished them from the old Australians.

The complex geography of Australia was a lesson in itself and an important lesson derived from our trips around the various states was the need to know about our own countries before going abroad as diplomatic representatives. I took that trouble on my return and utilised my first official leave to travel to unfamiliar areas. It turned out to be a timely action, as I was out on posting after only a year at headquarters.

Of course, traveling in Aussie land was much easier--wide-open spaces and expansive highways challenging the adventurous youthful driver. All you needed was a sturdy VW Beetle, few gallons of inexpensive fuel and one always found an excuse to hit the trail at weekends - Sydney and back to Canberra (400 miles), Melbourne and back (800 miles); in the end, weekend driving became a hobby, especially as we developed friendships beyond our training borders. In my case, having my wife and baby around provided a reason for taking them sightseeing.

After a christening ceremony of our baby, which involved a white South African godfather in the days of apartheid and an Australian godmother, I was able to return home after a year, which had transformed me from a provincial administrator into a fledgling diplomat.

I had to wait in those days. Unfortunately, we made the service so exclusive and special that it became attractive, the envy of the civil service in general and by persistent onslaught, our barriers were demolished, facilitating a general flow in both directions. Happily, the persistence of our successors has helped to reverse the situation. I hope it stops like this. With modest satisfaction, I recall that my predecessor as Permanent Secretary of the Ministry, HE Maurice Jones, and I engineered the process, which has virtually reestablished its original status. Foremost among our collaborators was Francis Karemo, who was brutally murdered with his wife by the rebels during their invasion of Freetown. May their gentle spirits rest in peace, in contrast to the eternal torment deserved by their killers.

I felt good to belong once more to an exclusive class of government officials, reminiscent of my spell at the Customs Department. This time, we were not known as civil servants or customs officers but by the appellation reserved for the super class of foreigners working locally for foreign governments and international institutions. If you had some knowledge of a foreign language among your credentials, you were even more special. A special status was and has always been awarded for foreign languages because of the linguistic parochialism within our educational system. Proficiency in Krio (the lingua franca), one or two indigenous languages and English (however impure) was considered adequate for popular or official communication. One cannot emphasize enough the need for corrective action in the linguistic education of our pupils and students. By feeding them with pre-digested chunks of whose ingredients they are unaware, we deprive them of the delightful opportunity of preparing their own recipes. The unfortunate outcome is that the majority of our students/graduates of today can hardly complete a statement or speech without violating the most basic rules of grammar. Given that improper use of grammar can distort the intended meaning of an expression, the student is often prone to misunderstand what he/she learns and therefore wrongly communicates that information. There is need for more emphasis on grammatical rules as the building blocks of communication!

In our day, we were encouraged to speak and write English correctly even at the elementary school level in preparation for secondary and tertiary refinement. Mistakes were noted and ridiculed while the perfectionists adopted the BBC diction as their standard. As English was and remains our official language and one of the major channels of international communication, it requires closer attention in our curriculum. French is, of course, a close second, since we are surrounded by so many francophone countries in our sub-region. The lingua franca, Krio, will no doubt retain its pride of place for local intercourse.

The Ministry's francophone deficiency was most evident in its earliest days as independent Sierra Leone welcomed teams from Guinea and other countries, and had to produce news releases and communiqués. Fortunately, there were a handful of young nationals who prioritised that language in their studies and Victor Summer, who had been a student in Quebec. As it happened, two of them, who turned out to be luminaries in their own right, became regular relief staff whenever the need arose. They were Patricia Tucker who later became First Lady Patricia Kabbah and Dr. Ramadan Dumbuya, who later became Foreign Minister. How much more exclusive can you get!

The emergence of a new species of officials at the disposal of the government blew a breath of fresh air into the work force. Young lawyers began to re-assess the prospect of a stereotyped daily procession into familiar courts of law or the sedentary confinement of a solicitor's office; general arts graduates visualised their professional prospects extending beyond humdrum desk-bound administration. Above all, the lure of spreading wings into foreign lands, which had been an exclusive hobby of the wealthy Sierra Leonean, was now a real possibility for the enterprising youngster. Even for non-diplomatic staff that would be needed as information and education attaches, drivers and secretaries, to activate and sustain embassies abroad, the temperature of expectation was running really high. In the circumstances, competition was also stiff, making it possible for only the best to be absorbed into what came to be regarded as an exclusive cadre. This perceived exclusivity turned out to be its Achilles heel. Ignoring the need for specialised training and the imperatives of performing flawlessly in the international areas, egalitarianism became the gospel of equalising through lowering instead of raising of standards. Thus, by onslaught from virtually every cadre of the civil service, the blue-eyed Foreign Service lost its special status but not its attraction. The rigorous requirements for admission were also maintained, however, and this not only disqualified but also discouraged adventurous aspirants and served as the lifeline that eventually facilitated return to the special status enjoyed at present.

Training was, and remains, a fundamental pillar for building and sustaining a reputable institution, especially for one that must stand the test of the highest international standards. Fortunately, the early builders of our external workforce recognised this and commenced training for its initial workforce even before they assumed duty. Much credit must be given to the older Commonwealth and their European friends, whose generosity made such opportunities available.

Probably through its own reverence for training, Sierra Leone was highly rated as a training destination. This is not a new accolade. In our early colonial history, Fourah Bay College became the regional training institution for Anglophone West African administrators, clerics, and teachers. Repeating history in a sense, the Ministry provided the bulk of a team training middle level diplomats from Anglophone West Africa. This programme was credible enough to be replicated for six consecutive years, only to be brought to an end by the civil war. One of the programme's proud achievements was that the Head of the Indian Foreign Service Training Institute, with our permission, took away our 6-week programme in Public Speaking. We can only hope that it had some influence on their curriculum. We would only be giving out some of the benefit we received from our benefactors.

The Ministry did not rest in neutral gear for long. Slowly but confidently moving forward, we soon had a presence at the United Nations as its hundredth member, established an embassy in Washington, a Consulate in New York, a High Commission in London and four West African missions in Conakry, Monrovia, Accra and Lagos.

Led by the vision, experience and drive of the first Foreign Minister, Dr. John Karefa-Smart, the image of the Ministry had every encouragement in its development. He had a previous international career to his belt and very cordial supportive relations with America through his academic and marital links. His Prime Minister, Sir Milton Margai, had similar links with Britain, which facilitated his assimilation among Commonwealth leaders. He was also reputedly a mild, peace-loving politician, who had steered our country to independence through cordial negotiations at Lancaster House rather than through violent confrontation as in Nkruma's Ghana.

The immediate post-independence image of 'Ancient and Loyal Sierra Leone' was the inevitable outcome of these antecedents. In the hands of loyalists, it was a bargaining chip for aid and other benefits, whilst for our critics, we were too ancient and subservient to our former colonial masters. On balance, we were more beneficiaries.

Taking up duty at the Ministry was such a new experience for an average administrative officer. Normally he would be hitched on to the monotony of a desk ad nauseam. In our case, we were rotated almost dizzily through the various sections-initially very few-to acquaint us with a holistic picture of the Ministry in preparation for posting to our new missions.

During my one-year induction, I even took charge of the Passports Section, which was issuing diplomatic passports until the task was handed over to the Immigration attaché posted to the Ministry and later relocated in the Immigration Department of the Sierra Leone Police.

Significantly, although these special passports are now issued by the Immigration Department for centralisation purposes, they are still processed through the Foreign Ministry.

Shuttling through the existing divisions allowed us to digest and adopt favourite ones because they were very few initially-- Administration, Political, International Organizations, Legal and Communications. These were not fully descriptive of their duties, but sufficed as headings - e.g. Admin included Protocol initially, and Political involved sensitising our missions abroad and linking them with one another through uniform bits of information from home and from each other. I was able to institute a bulletin for this purpose. This initiative and a fortuitous direct exposure to the Minister while in Administration initiated a process that catapulted me to the top of the Ministry in double quick time!

I happened to have prepared a draft for the Minister, which to everyone's surprise he approved without amendment. He identified me and promptly ordered my posting as Head of Chancery and First Secretary to Accra--the hub of Pan African politics--after one year in the Ministry.

9
Light from the Black Star

This was January 1963, when decolonization, African Liberation, African Unity and apartheid were top of the continental agenda. Preparations for the first OAU summit were being coordinated in Accra at full throttle and Nkrumah was the driver. To complicate matters for me, Africa was already visualised as a divided identity of the Cassablanca and Monrovia groups, with the former under the leadership of Kwame Nkrumah, whilst Sir Milton Margai and William Tubman typified the Monrovia group. As my High Commissioner was my former principal and chemistry teacher, I soon realised that the diplomatic burden was quite heavily tilted towards me. My strategy was to engage and befriend younger members of the African Affairs Secretariat, which had a profile even more prominent than the External Affairs Ministry. It was an exciting, stimulating but very challenging assignment. The enormous opportunity of meeting and discussing with Joshua Nkomo and other freedom fighters was like a tutorial for my later assignments at the UN, to which I will refer later. At the same time, I had to resist the temptations of the radical posture, which naturally infects youthful minds. At 30, I was vulnerable and impressionable, but Accra was relaxing enough to stabilise my professional restlessness.

One outstanding quality of the newly emancipated Ghanaians was the relaxed self-confidence with which they presented themselves. It spread an infectious aura over associates and critics alike and somehow, even the Sierra Leonean community, normally divisive and hypercritical at home, turned out to be a relaxed, positive and very supportive group. This facilitated my assignment tremendously.

Exposure to the intricacies of the evolving African geo-politics within its veritable cauldron was a privilege not available to many diplomats on their first posting. I recall the many instances when colloquia, rallies and special pre-OAU strategic meetings were being addressed in hyperbolic anti-colonial rhetoric by the likes of Nkomo (whom I got to know personally), ITA Wallace-Johnson, a firebrand compatriot with whom I had to fraternise privately while distancing myself publicly from his views. The Ghanaian experience proved to be a tutorial that benefited me and enriched my professional CV as a diplomat throughout that phase of my career. One memory that lingers was the funeral of W.E. Du Bois, where the African diplomatic corps processed to the graveside to be elevated by an oration delivered by Dr. Edward Wilmot Blyden III of Sierra Leone. It was comparable in style and effect to the rhetoric of Mark Anthony.

Ghanaians were also steeped in ceremonial. Being unaccustomed to so much cultural hypnosis at home, I was eager to enrich my experience at every opportunity. Even their landmarks had a special character about them. Accustomed to the brightness of stars, the new idea of the 'Black Star' was striking and unique. This uniqueness was further enhanced by erecting the Black Star Square as the focal point for all national activities. There was also the annual ogwira festival when all converged on the Aburi hills for fanfare, merriment and feasting on new yams and palm soup.

My cultural climax, however, was a visit to His Royal Highness, the Asantehene, Oba Agyeman, who was forbidden by tradition to travel across waterways of the sea. It was an eventual concession to modernisation, which broke the taboo of traveling across oceans. In reality, political friction necessitated his absence from the country for a while.

We bonded instantly. He explained the legend of the Ashanti stool, which was always guarded by a minor to preserve its innocence and purity. His umbrella was also ever present, complementing the golden decor that distinguished his regalia and paraphernalia and reflected the splendour of Ashanti land as a reservoir of gold.

Ghana was always very ceremonial anyway. The most distinguished ceremonial would lose its elegance and lustre if it was not floating in exotic local design of Kente cloth draped over one shoulder of the most venerable of gentlemen; whilst the women, in their buxom proportions, would bedeck themselves in wavy layers of Kente with matching head gear folded into exotic crowns, precariously perched, but never slipping off even in the most exotic African gyration.

In this setting, my first diplomatic assignment as administrative head of the High Commission was challenging but very pleasant. My kids interacted beautifully with their peers, learnt a few words/phrases in Twi and Ga and even learnt how to drape a Kente piece. Among the most significant and lasting features of this posting was the obvious eagerness of the newly emancipated Ghanaian to project the image of a dynamic African personality: the warm embrace and confident beaming smile had a missionary effect that closed gaps and forged effortless alliances.

With somewhat mixed feelings, I was suddenly uprooted from the Ghanaian experience just as it was profiling me for what I hoped would be the permanent career during my working life. It turned out, however, to be a fortuitous development. Apparently, the Foreign Minister, on his trip to the 1963 UN General Assembly, wanted a change of the staff in the Permanent Mission and instructed the Ministry to relocate me from Accra to New York immediately after the Assembly.

Without any previous experience of the New World, it was an exciting prospect, in spite of my reluctance to leave Accra.

10

New World: United Nations / State Department

After Accra, Australia, London, Durham and one or two European cities, I did not expect New York to be different, but it was! You were constantly surrounded by the shadows of gigantic sky-scrappers. Fortunately, the abundance of electricity ensured that neon lights brightened your path from dawn through dusk to dawn.

The speedy pace of life was also striking. Everyone was rushing past everyone else, almost like running to stay where you are. That first experience of Uncle Sam's paradise was overwhelming, but settling down was relatively easy because all systems seemed to be working smoothly.

Although my predecessor in the Mission had done his best to facilitate my accommodation and related arrangements, I soon discovered that no plans could be satisfactorily implemented in the office without the invisible but inevitable guiding hand of Pede Davies. He was as indispensable as he was unavoidable. He knew everyone and everything worth knowing.

Pede represented a trio of adventurous young Sierra Leonean workers, decently educated at the best secondary schools and poised to advance their education and fortunes in the New World. Harry Smythe and Peche Betts were already popular back home as athletes, whilst Harry's image was enhanced by association with his brother, Johnny, who was among the first African fighter pilots and a prisoner of war in the Second World War. Peche Betts was from an aristocratic family, producing citizens at the level of Chief Justice and Speaker of Parliament. The trio was a great help to young Sierra Leoneans settling down in a strange land. Pede, a Regentonian, was a young sporting legend in tennis, athletics and soccer. By virtue of a well-developed human relations skill, he acquired a very visible identity and a substantial constituency. His special constituency, however, was our diplomatic family and I recall quite fondly and gratefully, his invaluable contribution to my adjustment in an unfamiliar and challenging environment.

By virtue of being the seat of the United Nations, New York was in the mid-1960s, and probably still is, regarded as the capital of the world. By the time of arrival, I had tasted life in the UK and Australia, and sipped tasty drips of various Asian and African cultures, but New York was a special salad, incorporating ingredients from every conceivable garden. There was, in addition, the peculiar American flavour to virtually every incident.

I readily recall my first morning in the good old U.S.A. Entering the hotel cafeteria for breakfast, I ordered an omelet sandwich and a cup of coffee. In any other city of my previous visits, I would have been munching and sipping in a couple of minutes. This is not what happens in New York. The attendant first asked what type of bread: white, brown, wheat, rye, toasted, etc. While I was deciding, there was another barrage of questions about the coffee: cappuccino, expresso, black, white, decaf! All I recall is that I enjoyed a belly-warming treat before setting out on my first day's assignments.

Everyone posted straight from home is seen at first as being in need of a complete cultural orientation ceremony. Knowing of my previous exposure, however, limited mine to a minimum in the capable hands of Pede Davies.

Identifying and decorating an apartment in New York is like building a new house. This meant harnessing all activities, furniture and vehicle for the smooth execution of work (including entertainment), while also preparing for the reception of my family.

Then came the real assignment at the UN headquarters. The first discovery by a greenhorn in that diplomatic bazaar is that there is no room for apprenticeships. You are expected to arrive, ready for a full-time assignment, seasoned and prepared.

The perceptive newcomer is, of course, guided by the records of his Mission's performance, listens constructively and actively to interventions from traditional allies, and consolidates alliances in consonance with his country's established policies.

Our delegation had already found a niche in the Decolonisation Committee of 24 and the Apartheid Committee of 21 as well as the Committee on Peacekeeping expenses. The first two were straight forward, with guidelines already laid out by the Organisation of African Unity and for Africans and former colonised territories, and it was easy for all to sing in unison from the same hymn sheet. The Peacekeeping Expenses Committee turned out to be a cold war theatre where extreme caution had to be exercised by the non-aligned contingent, not wishing to upset and alienate either side. Eventually, they settled the dispute among themselves at the Security Council.

In the other two committees for which the Accra experience had fully equipped me, I was very comfortable and so the Permanent Representative made both my regular assignments.

The older members were probably tired of hearing each other's voices, and very ready to recruit me into the Resolutions drafting group and to be a presenter of the Resolutions. Being an eager debater, I embraced the opportunity with a zeal that got me into serious trouble a few months after my arrival.

Overflowing with confidence, I used hyperbolic language criticising British colonial behaviour. They were understandably incensed and reported me directly to Sir Milton Margai, the Prime Minister. Reputed for being "ancient and loyal" in his relations with the British, Sir Milton promptly ordered my recall. I was preparing my departure when I received the momentous news that plunged me into an emotional conflict.

The death of Sir Milton was a cause for national mourning by all Sierra Leoneans and I was no exception. As it turned out, that sad event also was a turning point in my diplomatic career, when I received a message from the new Minister instructing me to stay on and await the arrival of a new Ambassador.

Although no explanation was offered for my retention at my post, it appears that my statements were in tandem with our nation's new leadership. It was a deviation from the "ancient and loyal" era to the "Albert Margai of Africa" image. The new foreign minister, Cyril Rogers Wright, and the Permanent Representative, Gershom Collier, with whom I was already familiar, were known to be firebrands. In any case, it all worked out positively in my favour. The new Ambassador turned out to be Gershon Collier, who arrived and made me his blue-eyed boy. He worked hard, played hard and made us do the same.

Our interventions were always top of the pack, attracting delegates from large and small delegations for consultation. This was how I met and struck a strong friendship, which was eventually diluted by time and circumstance. Among the outcomes of that association were his chairmanship of my eldest daughter's wedding reception in London, his sponsorship for my membership of the Commonwealth club and our regular lunch whenever I passed through London. I refer to Emeka Anyaoku. He truly deserved his eventual elevation as Commonwealth Secretary General. I shall always cherish his friendship and inspiration.

At the U.N. Committee on Decolonisation with Ambassador Gershon Collier

The 1960s were hectic days in world politics, with the newly emancipated countries especially in Africa striving to carve out a significant niche for ourselves in a vigorously confrontational cold war environment. With the vibrant heat of the Cuban missile crisis threatening a nuclear explosion, the Security Council, a battle ground between entrenched blocks, the Peoples Republic of China (Peking) agitating vigorously for the elimination of Taiwan (Republic of China) from the geo-political world map, North and South Korea striving to eclipse each other, the Vietnamese war in incubation and Apartheid, Decolonisation and African Unity at the top of the African agenda, there was work for everyone.

Although our Mission staff in New York was minimal and the Permanent Representative doubled as Ambassador to Washington to reduce expenses, we were able to secure a non-permanent seat in the Security Council.

Dr. Davidson Nicol was also Director of the UN Institute for Training and Research (UNITAR) after serving as Sierra Leone's Permanent Representative at the United Nations, in succession to our former Chief Justice and President C. Okoro-Cole. Our discussions were meaty and incisive as we lingered over long drinks of 'planters punch' and other exotic concoctions in which I indulged experimentally.

It was in the midst of all these developments that the Nigerian bombshell hit us with the coup eliminating Sir Abubakar Tafawa Balewa culminating in the Biafran War.

After surviving my transfer scare from New York, I was now representing "Albert Margai of Africa" under the leadership of Ambassador Gershon Collier, an equally revolutionary visionary in Sir Albert's inner circle. I was considerably emboldened, and even though our main committees (24 and 21) were distinguished by senior luminaries, I managed to retain a prominent role among the spokespersons in crafting and presenting important Resolutions. Those luminaries included Natwar Singh of India, who later became a renowned author and Foreign Minister, and Malacela of Tanzania, who followed the same path. The New York experience was varied and thus very educative.

Being selected by the UN Secretariat to join a delegation to observe the decolonisation of Papua New Guinea was flattering but challenging.

The territory was really uncharted and the local folk in an almost primeval state. Semi-nudity was rampant. Apart from a limited local newssheet (New Guinea Tok Tok) printed in their current peculiar pidgin, there was no other evidence of literacy. Our hair raising experiences in one-engine planes flying in narrow ravines between two hill tops were more lasting and even upon recollection 50 years later, I am losing a heart-beat.

The comforting thought is that following that visit, the territory's march towards self-government gained momentum. The trip was hazardous, but successful. For me, personally, there was the bonus of visiting Australia once more, meeting old friends and being welcomed to the "Refugees Club."

The New York posting was an enlarging experience not fully realised at the time. Being enlisted in Columbia University's 1965 Calendar as "Part-time lecturer on African Affairs" was personally flattering, but mainly due to Sierra Leone's rising profile in the UN system. Opportunities were even offered for international advancement when a UN Under-Secretary General invited me to lunch and asked me to be his Personal Assistant. Unhappy about the prospect of losing my services, Ambassador Gershon Collier discouraged me, arguing that the sky would be the limit for me in our national service and that the nation needed me. I was influenced by the patriotic appeals, especially when my Ambassador accompanied me to a second lunch appointment with the same Under-Secretary General. To be honest, my life as a professional diplomat had its good points but never realised the expectations and promise of Gershon Collier and myself.

It has to be admitted that an assignment at the UN is probably the crowning glory of a diplomat's career because of the variety, complexity and volume of situations encountered.

In response to this, the larger missions rely on specialists operating in the various committees and sub-committees concentrating on the various issues. These are specialised mechanisms to facilitate the organisation's work. The multiplicity of committees obviously imposes great strain on smaller missions, where numbers are inadequate and specialists in short supply. Missions like ours, therefore, had to produce jacks-of-all-trades and masters of few.

Operating in interest groups was a convenient tactic. We operated mainly within the African Group and the Non-aligned group. Rotational chairmanship gave them an egalitarian aura but having to chair a full meeting of Ambassadors and other Heads of Mission in the absence of my Ambassador was quite a handful. Fortunately, he was seldom out of post on home consultation.

Incidentally, New York was not all the labourer's task. The exotic trips to the top of the Empire State building, the Statute of Liberty on Staten Island, a rare evening listening to Gladys Knight at the Waldorf, James Brown at Small's Paradise or the New York Philharmonic, were choice items on the menu. Driving for miles in the mid-town tunnel, knowing you are surrounded by water, also has its special thrills; similarly, strolling through Central Park not knowing what to expect at any minute was exciting! All this was New York, far from home and local culture. We also devised our own leisure activities. The group entertainment was less of an 'awojor' but certainly a feast in semi-African style. Our mission also had its fair share of West Indians from Trinidad and Jamaica plus a flamboyant Puerto Rican, who made everyone realise he was 'the Ambassador's driver'! With the odd West African also in our midst, our ambience in and out of the office was visibly positive.

Upon reflection, its seems as if I spent several years instead of only 20 months in New York, considering the scope of my involvement in its turbulence.

My movement took me to Washington DC instead of homewards as one would expect, but I did not mind that alternative as it enlarged my experience in one or two ways. First, the assignment concentrated on regular diplomatic administration for which my tour in Accra had prepared me. Secondly, American diplomatic practice was revered around the world and worth experiencing by any diplomat. For those of us trained in the

Western tradition, it was the ultimate posting. In addition, I was available from Washington to fly or drive the 200 miles to New York to augment the Mission especially during the three-month session of the UN General Assembly.

Frankly, I was missing Sierra Leone already; I therefore took my family home leave before my new post to Washington D.C.

Unlike New York, I had no Pede Davies to welcome and chaperon me. I, therefore, went out, on my first Saturday, to buy extras for our furnished house before the family's arrival. It was a bright and sunny but surprisingly cold afternoon. However, the biggest surprise was yet to come. As I drove home, a freak snowstorm engulfed Washington, and in half an hour, I had to abandon my car only to have my hair studded with freezing solidified snowflakes. The pain was excruciating.

My next memorable experience of DC was a visit to the White House as Charge d'Affaires, when we were there to meet the King of Saudi Arabia. The magnificent organisation was faultless and breathtaking.

In later years, whilst visiting Saudi Arabia with President Siaka Stevens, it struck me that, allowing for the difference between European and Arabic cultures, they were neck to neck in magnificence and splendour.

President Lyndon Johnson turned out to be a very pleasant and hospitable host, inviting us on a trip to his ranch in Texas, where I saw horses and riders in breathtaking manoeuvres. Official life in Washington was relatively unruffled and certainly less hectic than the hustle and bustle of New York. Our challenges were more consular but of a different kind from New York, which ran a high-powered consular office for trade and business. Washington had responsibility for our nationals, visa issues and most of all our numerous students throughout the United States and Canada.

What welcome chance this provided to see the country, its educational variety and its economic and cultural variety. My love for traveling (especially driving) made me an easy target to deputise my Ambassadors at University functions countrywide, since they invariably had a double accreditation to the Embassy and the Permanent Mission. This arrangement suited me practically, as I had the official Cadillac at my disposal and was largely left to operate it unsupervised. This arrangement also built up my confidence and undoubtedly prepared me for my next assignment, which will be revealed later and turned out to be the most risky and demanding episode of my diplomatic career.

My last days in Washington nearly blighted my diplomatic prospects, as the new Ambassador and I disagreed over instructions I considered unprofessional. As we were both uncompromising, the Ambassador referred his case to the Head of State, a military Brigadier and my Ministry, requesting my return to Freetown and exclusion from the General Assembly delegation due in a month. In response, I copied my version of events to both destinations, but this did not save me initially. The Ministry recalled me in accordance with the Ambassador's recommendation. After a month of my earned leave in London, I returned home, requested and was granted audience with the Head of State who, to my surprise and relief, applauded my stand, and ordered my return to the General Assembly for its three-month duration.

Although I felt vindicated, reprieved and relieved, I must offer a note of caution to staff who may find themselves in similar situations. Your case must be watertight, ethically and legally, and presented with transparent simplicity. The feelings of the superiors should also be constantly in mind and every effort made to refrain from gloating or any appearance of it.

In my ease, I enlisted the assistance of the Permanent Secretary to appease the Ambassador, notified the mission of my arrival whilst en route (to minimise a resistant attitude) and had a luncheon arranged soon after arriving, to establish a conducive social climate for the session. It worked. A significant outcome of this experience was that when I became Permanent Secretary of the Ministry, I got my Ministers to agree that disputes between Ambassadors and their staff should not be decided automatically by recalling the staff member. The matter should be investigated and both should be assisted to reconcile their differences and continue to work amicably. This is less expensive and contributes to the smooth performance and cohesive image of the Ministry. It did not take root immediately, but after I had tactfully challenged or circumvented the transfer instructions given to me for three successive recalls it became standard practice.

With the Washington/New York episode behind me, I was on my way to a peaceful spell at home when someone whispered, as I stopped over in London, that an important posting was awaiting me on arrival in Freetown.

11
The Nigerian Crucible

As it turned out, a herculean task awaited me. I had been earmarked to re-open and head our High Commission in Lagos. Financial constraint had dictated its closure a few years earlier, but with the Biafran war in full swing, numerous Sierra Leoneans at risk on both sides of the conflict, our diplomatic presence was considered necessary and urgent.

In Lagos, a High Commissioner's residence was under construction but could not be completed for occupancy until eight months after my arrival. Fortunately, there was an affordable junior suite at the Federal Palace Hotel, which became my home during that period. It afforded little privacy for a mission's operations, but it was comfortable and in the absence of domestic chores, which were efficiently managed by a caring and conscientious hotel staff, life was reasonably smooth.

A very professional maitre d'hotel offered sympathetic service by preparing occasional dishes outside of the regular official menu, and this provided variety to a monotonous existence.

The Nigerian assignment was an acid test evoking responses at various levels. Although I had a loyal and competent Head of Chancery in the person of Alhaji Seray-Wurie for consultation, I was now, unlike my previous position, the ultimate arbiter in an unusual civil war scenario.

My entire stay in Nigeria was virtually circumscribed by the Biafran rebellion and characterised by various related factors.

- Sierra Leoneans were widely dispersed across both sectors of the rebellion with the Biafran residents desiring and expecting evacuation as living conditions worsened.

- The Nigerian government was expecting 100 percent sympathy and support based on its traditional friendship with Sierra Leone.
- Biafra was gaining sympathetic allies from regions outside Africa as well as African governments outside the sub-region, whose ties with Nigeria were more fragile.
- The powerful nature of the Biafra propaganda machine was enhanced by the degree of deprivation and suffering that had reduced them to feeding on lizards.
- This propaganda was swaying Sierra Leone in their favour and complicating my work in the process, as my assignment was to maintain and improve relations with Nigeria.

Several factors on the ground were exploited to this end. The media had a recognisable Sierra Leone component, which was carefully cultivated, and the sympathetic Nigerian component was incorporated tactfully to enhance presentation of the Nigeria-Sierra Leone friendship. The Fourah Bay College alumni around the country were organised into an alliance of sympathisers.

It also proved useful to project the Missions' representative into the public eye by infiltrating prominent society as much as possible. In this regard, prominent Sierra Leonean descendants proved very useful.

The Mayor of Lagos, Chief Bakari, warmly embraced me and drove me around in his convertible Cadillac on the odd evening; and the Governor of Lagos State, of Sierra Leonean ancestry, would welcome me and the British High Commissioner to carpet bowls at his residence after an evening of tennis with diplomats and Foreign Service officials.

The American Ambassador's tennis parties clinched a personal friendship, whilst prominent politicians like TOS Benson and social professionals like Dr. Simi Johnson complemented our alliance.

My personal programme is not a standard schedule for all diplomats, but I hope it will provide a few guidelines for a young professional who is preparing a work plan in a new station. A diplomat must be affable, informed, persuasive, mentally agile, and always focused on the interest of his or her country. In a situation fraught with conflicting alternatives, it is advisable to critically examine all possible options before deciding on the most advantageous or the least disadvantageous to your nation's interest. In the Nigerian Biafra conflict, the main options appeared to be:

Supporting Nigeria to the hilt to preserve the integrity of the Federal Republic.

or

Expressing/displaying sympathy towards the weaker side in a visibly uneven contest and consequently persuading the stronger side (the Federation) to make concessions.

With our nationals widely dispersed on both sides, we had to walk on a tight rope. With the help of foreign agencies like the International Red Cross, evacuation from the besieged East was facilitated, but the stories of their suffering, on reaching home, heightened sympathy for the cause of Biafra as the underdogs.

This complication positioned me to underplay the sympathy card in order to maintain our friendship with the Federal Republic. Many will recall the acronym 'GOWON' for "GO ON WITH ONE NIGERIA", which was also the name of the Head of State, General GOWON.

Thus, I became entangled in a tussle between a sympathetic government at home, on the one hand, and a host Nigeria government where suspicion of our loyal friendship was germinating.

Sierra Leone Foreign Minister Brewah, with high-powered delegation, local and foreign dignitaries visiting my High Commission in Lagos

My connections with Eastern Nigeria (Biafra) were quite strong, with my middle name, Onyeah, offering clear evidence. I was also fairly certain that the Nigerian Government knew that the wife of the Biafran Chief Justice (Mrs. Mbanefo) was the sister of my mother-in-law. My movement, comments and attitudes thus had to be very guarded. Portraying neutrality was not enough. I was expected by the host Government to be transparently sympathetic, whilst growing sympathy for Biafra noises from our Parliament and the press was in the air. This attitude was contrary to my own assessment. The result was a fierce barrage of persuasive correspondence directed not only to my Ministry but also sent directly to State House for the personal attention of President Siaka Stevens. Those Post Reports succeeded in delaying any precipitous pro-Biafran action but, eventually, at the end of my assignment in November 1969, the local politicians prevailed and Parliament adopted a Resolution to recognise Biafra. Fortuitously, the war ended before the Resolution could be publicised and applied.

I have often wondered how many Nigerian soldiers would have agreed to come over and die during our own rebel war, if we had recognised Biafra.

I often thank the Almighty for his inspiration and guidance in that predicament and, lest I forget, it is instructive to mention that unorthodox measures like arranging periodic jam sessions with Geraldo Pino's band set to entertain off-duty Nigerian soldiers and Sierra Leonean nationals helped to synthesise inter-country relations!

Although the war and its repercussions dominated our official focus, no one in that position could afford to ignore the vast variety in the life and customs of the continent's most populous country. In spite of the war, it was, indeed, a rich reservoir of cultures, involving legends, practices and artifacts, all embedded in an enigmatic maze of wise reflective perception and often entangling diction. The "parable" was invariably the wisest and most common means of transmitting knowledge and the wisdom of the ages. I availed myself of these golden opportunities at every opportunity. Such memories included a special visit to His Royal Highness, the Olubadan of Ibadan. There, I was regaled with stories of Shango, the God of Fire, and the inexorable consequence of challenging or violating his edicts or authority. Thanks to that visit, which included the University and the Governor of the State, one of my priceless diplomatic mementos is a bronze effigy of an Olubadan of Ibadan.

In Benin City, the Oni of Ife was a highly intelligent and affable ruler. He opened up to me so completely that when he left me alone in the room to fetch some photographs, I felt a bit sweaty and proceeded to open two windows, not realising I was looking down into his harem--a privilege strictly permitted only to a husband. I did not see more than a few pairs of eyes but he was very tactful in relieving my embarrassment.

In the North, Kano and Maiduguri were beautiful specimens of Oriental (Arabic) civilisation, featuring the walled city in Kano, a skyline of minarets and a breathtaking durbar combining equestrian agility with elegance.

The persistent legacy of my Nigerian experience has been the friendship I have enjoyed with several nationals whom I assisted to return home as refugees.

I will also be doing a great disservice to the Nigerian Head of State, General Yakubu Gowon, during whose regime I served, if I fail to recount two significant encounters I had with him personally.

As the diplomatic corps stood in single file to welcome a visiting Head of State at the airport, General Gowon guided the visitor and they both shook hands with all the Ambassadors. It started drizzling as he approached me as the senior of the acting

Heads. Understandably, he waved to me as they hurried past. To my utter surprise and admiration, when we all assembled at His residence on his wedding day, as the ladies were struggling to keep their hats from being blown away by the helicopters' whirlwind, the General shook my hand, accepted my congratulations and said he was sorry for appearing to ignore me at the airport--two weeks earlier. I was virtually speechless--a rare experience.

On another occasion, at the Commonwealth Summit in Canada, which I attended with President Siaka Stevens, I was standing beside the officials' garage waiting for my vehicle when General Gowon emerged at the adjacent Heads of State entrance. He saw me about 50 yards away, said "Hello" and took a few steps towards me.

Understandably, I warmed up into an early morning sprint, towards him. He shook my hand, enquired what I was now engaged in, and when I replied that I was then Permanent Secretary of Foreign Affairs, he congratulated and encouraged me. Here was an officer and a gentleman, who will always stand out in my memory.

Another personality who was similarly admirable, professionally and personally was Olu Adeniji. He had endeared himself to Sierra Leone in his early diplomatic career on posting to their High Commission in Freetown. He cemented his relationship by marrying a lady of Sierra Leonean extraction but preserved his Yoruba identity by ensuring that his entire family--self, spouse and siblings had "Olu" names. During my tenure, he was my tennis mate and facilitated my relations with the Foreign Ministry. On his later assignment to Sierra Leone as the UN Secretary General's Special Representative during our Rebel War, we renewed our relationship personally and officially.

12
Dizzy Heights

Diplomats tend to look forward to postings abroad, lured by the prospect of representation allowance, but even more by the anticipation of exposure to foreign customs and the variety of new experiences by which they may feel enlarged.

On the contrary, in spite of the superficial elitism and surrealistic affluence surrounding the diplomatic identity, the homeward call filters through to most of us after a few years on posting. In my case, after four significant postings (Accra, New York, Washington, and Lagos) over a period of 7 years (Jan 1963 - Dec 69), home was a welcome change. Little did I expect, however, that the heaviest load was awaiting me in the Ministry. Within months of my arrival, the two officers senior to me at post were transferred/elevated to other MDAs and with the approval of Cyril Foray, the Minister, I was promoted Permanent Secretary. There were other officers of comparable seniority but comfortably lodged at outposts. Fortuitously, Cyril Foray and I were Durham originals and our mutual regard facilitated our official relationship.

I could not readily foresee the herculean dimension of the Permanent Secretary's assignment but it was not long before all was revealed. A significant feature of this period was the emerging fever of Republicanism, with the expectation of complete political freedom from colonialism. A local President answerable only to his people and enjoying their ultimate allegiance was the Utopian desire of the politicians; no more the intermediary of a post-colonial Governor General for governance decisions to be confirmed by Whitehall. In this process, foreign relations would be enhanced and expanded and the inherited focus on the

Commonwealth augmented by a worldwide range of international alliances. Even Sir Banja Tejan-Sie and Sir Salako Benka-Coker were subject to such restrictions.

Within a few months of my tenure, my assignment was to preside (as Master of Ceremonies) at the inauguration of our First Executive President, Dr. Siaka Probyn Stevens. At this point, he was understandably sensitive about his image and that of the country. This was particularly evident in the detailed programme for the inauguration ceremony, to which neighbouring Heads of State were invited. Following on the heels of an attempt on his life, it was a bold move to guarantee security to visiting Heads. President Sekou Toure, who was himself besieged by domestic intrigues, sent his Prime Minister, Beavogue, but President Tolbert of Liberia was present. With only one Head of State, security was, of course, easier to handle.

This must have been the first time that the 'poro' society operated publicly in Freetown and for non-members like myself, the deafening thunderous rumble they produced has been a life-long memory.

It would be an understatement to describe Sierra Leone's international experience in the 1970s as just eventful. This was the era of our personhood expansion in various dimensions. Freed from the restrictive influence of the colonial heritage and our univocal pro-western perception, we were ready to see and embrace a new multi-dimensional international landscape. One of the important issues was the recognition of the People's Republic of China (Peking) to replace the Republic of China (Taiwan) as the legitimate claimants to seats in the UN General Assembly and the Security Council. This was perhaps the most momentous move of that era but there were other dilemmas to be resolved, like the adjustment to two Koreas, a more open relationship with communist regimes like Russia, China and Cuba, resulting in the opening of embassies.

Laying Wreath at Lenin's Tomb in Moscow, with Foreign Minister Solomon Pratt, Ambassador Edward Blyden and my Secretary Meliora

In spite of the Arab-Israeli conflict and the former's influence within the OAU, an Israeli embassy was inevitable, especially, with their tremendous business capability, which materialised in their building of our Parliament with almost every item imported from Israel.

Sections of this overview presentation will be unfolded later but in the earliest stages of the Republic, the visit of Emperor Haile Selassie stands out as a most significant diplomatic scoop.

Late in 1971, with what seemed like insufficient notice, I was entrusted with the onerous but dignified duty of organising the visit for February 1972. My political reference was S.I. Koroma, the Vice President, who updated me on the President's wishes and preference for the programme, but gave the Ministry a completely free hand in the arrangements and provided the funds we needed. One example of this is that we sometimes extended our working hours until almost midnight, but were free to order dinner from the Paramount Hotel--accounted for of course! More significantly, we were probably the first institution apart from the Security Agencies to import and use a walkie-talkie system. With the aid of the High Commission in London, the whole transaction from the Ministry's catalogue identification to testing in Freetown took about a week.

With the elite corps of officers at my disposal, I felt confident that nothing could go wrong. What a team! Gustavus Williams, Eya Mbayo, John Bankole-Jones, Sylvanus Taylor, Victor Sumner, Sahr Matturi, Joseph Koroma, Francis Karemo, Charles Wyse, Freddie Savage and Etien Dupigny, the communications officer who was always on duty.

In case one is misled into thinking we were an all-male contingent, I must emphasise that the female contingent was equally elitist: Jeredine Williams, Caroline Koroma, Dunstanette Williams, Gertrude Sheriff were a perfect match and in symbiotic liaison with their male counterparts.

Actually, in spite of all this hype, something did go wrong but it was not their fault. For general interest, it is worth recounting.

Emperor Haile Selassie, who was always in his military uniform, sent us an impressive photo depicting his immaculate Royal Majesty's military uniform.

State House in Freetown, on the other hand, gave us an elegant photograph of our civilian President in an immaculate suit. Frankly, our President never looked more attractive.

94

On the front cover of the official programme, both photographs faced each other. However, the printing was only completed in the morning of the Emperor's arrival, as the photographs arrived late. Only the bare programme had been vetted and approved earlier by State House. The souvenir copies were delivered by the Printing Department on the morning of the visit and President Stevens was given a copy by his Secretary on their way to the airport. He then recalled that there was a recent photo of himself as Commander in Chief in the new and very impressive red and black officers' uniform.

I nearly froze when the SPs voice bellowed over my receiver that H.E. was livid and wanted his military photograph on the programme. This was one occasion when a delay proved a blessing. All the remaining copies had just been assembled awaiting collection from the Printing Department.

A lightning dispatch of my most dynamic lady, Jeredine, with instructions to supervise the change proved effective. Another glow of good fortune was the delay of the Emperor's flight, which arrived two hours late. I informed neither the Secretary nor H.E. of the change. You can imagine, therefore, their surprise on arrival at the National Stadium to receive the amended copies. I watched the President as his controlled frown melted into an uncontrolled smile. Little wonder that he ordered a special letter of commendation to me after the visit. My staff and I received and celebrated the honour as only diplomats can. This State visit was an assignment I enjoyed from a professional viewpoint, as I was emotionally shattered by the loss of my sister, a member of my household, on the morning of the Emperor's arrival.

The return visit of our President to the Emperor was even more eventful. I left for Addis Ababa a few days ahead of the delegation in order to liaise and oversee the arrangement. Our national insignia had just arrived and President Stevens wanted to make a mark by conferring national honours on the Emperor and some senior officials. Consequently, an assortment of our insignia from the Bank of Sierra Leone vault, neatly laid in a small suitcase, was entrusted to me, traveling alone without any security. Changing flight in Accra, the case, which had been forcibly confined to the hold, was missing!

I stayed in Accra for two days, anxiously monitoring every arriving flight, requested State House to assemble a replacement package whilst I activated all airport communication lines along the route. On my third day, despondent but hopeful, I saw a mountain of luggage from an arriving plane with my little red suitcase at the apex. Usain Bolt, however fast he bolted, would have been a distant second as I rushed to the tarmac, ordered it to be handed over on the spot and carried it for verification. Since the bulk of airport staff already knew and sympathised with my plight, we were all relieved. I could imagine the relief at State House when I cancelled my request. That very night, I left for Addis with my valuable suitcase in the Cabin. A generous draught of cognac and a sound sleep restored my equilibrium. The visit was fantastic. With liveried waiters in a fairy tale presentation, lavish cuisine and cutlery in gleaming gold, it was and is my most elegant banquet ever. Lunch with the Queen and Prince Phillip in the Great Hall was of course a special treat for the only African student in the Hall of Durham because he happened to be President of the prestigious Union Society.

Among the benefits of the Ethiopian visit was the decoration of our President and senior officials in national honours. My good fortune landed me with "Commander of the Order of Menelik II".

Addis Ababa had its beautiful allure as well as its hazards. An elegant and hospitable people, soft-spoken but hard-working, in spite of its remarkable height above sea level, it is little wonder that they are so outstanding in overcoming the rigorous demands of marathons.

For hapless foreigners like us from the lowlands, it was, however, a different experience. The first and second floors of a hotel were our constant preference, especially after hearing that a West African had collapsed while climbing to the penthouse.

Being the seat of the OAU and the Economic Commission for Africa, it enriched the knowledge and experience of a wide range of diplomats and officials in constant procession to the Emperor's capital.

Back at headquarters, I realised that minor gear adjustments were necessary for smooth liaison with each Foreign Minister.

Cyril Foray, a historian, was quite intellectual, relaxed, discourse-oriented and receptive. With youthful intellectuals around him, work was a pleasure for all. At conferences, meetings and in general interaction, he was an excellent speaker but also a good listener.

Solomon Pratt (aka Jolly boy), an equally intellectual product, was generally identified by the boundless range of his professional interests and his inexhaustible physical energy. I recall that during the extensive travels I undertook with him to conferences and official visits, he was busy preparing, single-handed, the draft of one of our national constitutions.

Desmond Luke was elitist, punctilious and highly principled. Being an Oxford Blue was evidence of his physical strength, but this was neatly encased in his unruffled exterior, but when confronted with a breach of some fundamental principle, a volcano erupted. As an example, he is the only cabinet Minister who has resigned because State House flouted the principle of precedence in presenting Ambassadorial credentials. He was, nonetheless, respected enough to be appointed Chief Justice in a subsequent administration.

In my interaction with Ministers, I discovered that they preferred administrators with backbones, if only the latter were prepared to carry their own share of problems and be persuasive without confrontation.

Three examples stand out in my recollection:

- While in New York at the General Assembly with Solomon Pratt, someone brought a complaint to the Minister against one of our officers in the mission. Jolly Boy was incensed, prepared a telegram for me to dispatch to the President requesting the officer's immediate recall. I persuaded him that it was a matter for me to resolve and it was so resolved. This officer became one of the best Directors-General the Ministry has produced.

- Desmond Luke asked me to recall an officer who was in conflict with his Ambassador at post. Having been an Ambassador himself, his approach was understandable, but I convinced him that (i) it was better to resolve their differences and work amicably thereafter; (ii) that the officer is not always wrong and the case should be investigated; and (iii) it would be too expensive to effect transfers whenever disputes arose. "O.K. P.S." was his brief concession and that was the beginning of a new approach to personality or policy conflicts at our missions abroad.

- Francis Minah rather selectively instructed me to recall two officers from major missions on grounds I could not justify in good conscience. One was a cardiac implant patient but working excellently. I argued that since the mission was happy and transfer may endanger his life, he should remain at his post. He did. The other was Minah's professional colleague who was making efforts to improve his qualification through evening classes in his own time and at his own expense. The Minister had been told he was using office hours for classes, but I was able to disprove this and the officer even got his doctoral degree ultimately.

I had equally smooth sessions during my brief assignments with Sembu Forna and Sani Sesay in the Ministries of Agriculture and Mines respectively.

On the basis of my own experience, my advice to Permanent Secretaries is to be tactful but self-confident and interact positively with your political heads. They expect and value your guidance, even if they do not admit it.

Admit it or not, your Ministry is special; at least, it was so special in my day that whenever my Minister was out of the country, President Siaka Stevens took over the Ministry and I became his Permanent Secretary. I have to admit that the rapport we developed during these sessions proved useful in other ways and landed me in a few unusual assignments and experiences.

On two occasions, I was assigned to settle difficult problems in neighboring countries. Recovery of a fishing vessel seized by Guinea was relatively challenging but turned out successfully after a week of interviews and contacts together with my friend, Eya Mbayo, who was Acting Head of Mission in

Guinea. The vessel sailed smoothly homeward while we spent the weekend mopping up relations.

At the other border, our police officer had strayed into Liberian territory and got himself arrested and detained, where upon I was assigned to go and rescue him. The task seemed rather complex but, fortunately, the Liberian Foreign Minister was newly appointed on his return from Freetown, where he was Secretary-General of the Mano River Union. It was in his interest to lubricate relations with us, and as we had become acquainted in that institution, I had no problems. However, my visit became complicated on the day of my arrival by the sad news of the death of President V.S. Tubman, whose corpse was being flown from abroad that day for burial in state. I had to wait and join our delegation to be led by the Vice President Hon. S. I. Koroma. It was a grand, solemn and memorable historical experience, which bonded me to "S.I." and led to two other official visits to Liberia by the two of us.

My very special assignment from President Stevens was the unexpected designation of Special Envoy to the Gulf States as Head of a 5-man delegation to solicit development assistance in the Minerals, Energy, and Aviation and Transportation sectors. The result was a handsome cash offer followed by project evaluation missions on the specified areas. For a professional diplomat, it was an invaluable experience and very satisfying personally.

Upon reflection, my liaison with President Stevens had its slightly bumpy interludes. His insistence on having me as a member of all his delegations was sometimes destabilising. I recall the instance when I returned from an inspection in Cairo, reported at State House where the Minister was waiting for me, only to be pulled aside and told that H.E. would be leaving next morning and wanted me on his delegation. It was a pleasant trip but quite demanding on me physically. He left me out of only one OAU Summit in Lomé, but compensated by appointing Mrs. Farma Joka Bangura and myself to participate as Head of Delegation and Foreign Minister at a subsequent meeting when election fever was at its height locally.

President Stevens: Local Political Icon

Even when he met the UN Secretary General at the UN in New York, only three of us were present--the President, the Permanent Representative Dr. Edward Blyden III and myself. Looking at the Perm Rep iconic photograph preserved in his memoirs, we were like three rungs of a ladder: the Perm Rep and U Thant were the same height while I stood between them and H.E. A sumptuous private dinner concluded that memorable visit.

One of the lasting legacies of the liaison was the practice of speech writing for H.E. in conjunction with His Secretary Mr. G.L.V. Williams. With only the two of us on this assignment, it was uniquely demanding.

My swansong in this regard was H.E.'s closing address to the OAU Summit in Freetown. Although I was engaged in WARDA, Sierra Leone's Foreign Minister, Abdulai Conteh, invited me to assist in the administration of the OAU Conference alongside Victor Summer, then Permanent Secretary. The visit of Emperor Haile Selassie and this conference were high points of President Stevens' Executive Presidency and must be well remembered.

13
Cultivating the Sub-Region

Despite the growing perception of the global village, disparities were not likely to embrace us within the fold. Smaller States, in fact, felt even more isolated within the village, especially as bigger, more prosperous states were consolidating separate economic and geopolitical groups, alienating, or at best differentiating, themselves from the new members of the "village." In this context, the emergence of the Mano River Union as a sub-regional organisation at the initial stage of our Republic, reflected some positive thinking on the part of our leader, Siaka Stevens. Its present composition including Cote d'Ivoire is a testament to its sub-regional influence.

Personally, I feel privileged to have been involved as Director of Finance and Administration in the plans and the event of the official opening of the Mano River Bridge linking Liberia and Sierra Leone. As we walked behind both Presidents across the bridge from one country to the other, many of us could not help feeling that we were making a modest contribution to regional solidarity and, by extension, to international relations.

In good and bad times, the Union is an inevitable link. During the devastating rebel wars in Sierra Leone and Liberia, the whirlwind sucked in the Republic of Guinea among the liberating forces.

Similarly, when peace and tranquility returned, the smooth flow of cross-border trade and reunification of kinsfolk brought happiness, reviving prosperity to the region needing rejuvenation. Soothing as this may sound, it must never be allowed to dilute the agony of the preceding days of strife, rebellion and destruction.

Let the gruesome experience of conflicts serve, instead, as a constant rebuke to our neighbours and beyond, never to stray along that path of self-destructive civil war! A fitting 'In Memoriam' at this point would be to recall with much sorrow the sad fate of Dr. Cyril Bright, the first Secretary-General of the Union, who also became one of the first victims of the upheaval in Liberia. He was executed by firing squad on a beach in Monrovia, merely for being a Minister--a position he flatly declined and was forced to accept for a short while. What a tragedy.

In spite of the different colonial experiences of the Union's membership, that diverse heritage of French culture in Guinea, American influence in Liberia, and British tutelage in Sierra Leone has given way to enthusiastic collaboration in the furtherance of their collective interest.

The excursion into West Africa Rice Development Association (WARDA) was an unexpected break from Civil Service routine but the experience was worthwhile, reminding me of my Mano River Union assignment, and more comprehensive

Following my pattern of unexpected transition from one job to another, Dr. Harry Will, who was the Director of Research in WARDA Headquarters in Monrovia, suddenly appeared in my office in Freetown and informed me of a vacancy for a Director. He brought an application form, which I completed for him to take back. I was pleased to be selected from among 15 candidates and will always acknowledge a debt of gratitude to Harry for his confidence in me and persistent support in my assignment.

The West Africa Rice Development Association seemed like a blossom from the Mano River Union seedling. An organisation embracing all the countries of the West African sub-region was fraught with challenges. Chief among these was its variety of indigenous and imposed cultures, languages, currencies and natural resources. The commodity of common interest was, however, strong enough to justify cooperation, as rice was and still is the main food crop in the entire sub-region.

Performing duties in a capacity similar to my MRU experience was deceptively attractive, but it soon became clear that their problems superseded their common interest. For me personally, managing personnel from a wide variety of nationalities could have been more stressful, but the experience of the U.N. Mission had prepared me to manage multinationals. From outside the sub-region, the Association had highly qualified professional staff within my administration, whose support helped to reduce the effect of regional or national jealous tendencies. Overarching our operations also was a Resident Representative of the Food and Agricultural Organization (FAO) under whose auspices and conditions we were operating.

With all these safeguards, there remains the common threat, which tends to cripple multinational associations of third world states (i.e. finance). There was ample international support for the Association around the world, with provision for personnel training, and economic and scientific research by a solid reservoir of international experts in constant consultation.

In such a salubrious setting, the only fly in the ointment was the obligation of Member States to pay for the administrative cost of the Organisation. Their inability to fulfill this vital chore led to the eventual dismantling of my department and return to the Civil Service of my Government for my final three years.

Six years in Monrovia at WARDA's head office was not without its memorable incidents. I was there, for example, when their upheaval erupted! It was on a public holiday when all of Monrovia was relaxed and I was among the foreigners who had chosen the night for an interactive dinner. The journey home proved to be beyond our wildest expectations. Five individuals of mixed nationality in my vehicle driving serenely by the Executive Mansion were suddenly jolted from our holiday dream by a motley band of soldiers, apparently drugged, shouting "Halt!" Therefore, we did. Approaching us with an aggressive deployment around our vehicle, the identifiable leader proclaimed without any obvious emotion "We have just killed Tolbert. We are now the Government!" All of us froze instantly.

At that moment, I whispered to everyone to remain silent as I put on the lights in the car, opened the door and stood with one foot on the road. Seconds later, we heard a gunshot around the rear of my car. This turned out to be one of the soldiers who aimed a shot at my rear tire at 6 paces... and missed. Somehow, the vehicle was not immobilised, but this bullet landed in my brake drum and had to be removed later in the repair shop.

Upon later reflection, the danger of that gunshot really dawned on us. The stray bullet could have landed in the back seat where three of my passengers were leaning on each other. What a potential tragedy. From another angle, the brake drum could have sent metal splinters on to my left leg resting on the road. By Divine Grace, neither scenario happened. Incidentally, on hearing the gunshot from the rear, I could have turned round to see what was happening, but I did not want to lose the attention of the bosses talking to me at the front-end. Calmness was my best option with an appropriate comment, "Thank you for the information gentlemen. Our duty now is to go home and listen to the message you want us to send to our governments."

Giving them time to shut the car door after I sat down, I waived them goodbye and drove off very slowly before turning off the cabin lights. My next hurdle was dropping off all four passengers before driving home.

In this entire incident, I was really saved by special Divine favour. The coupists did not know that among my passengers was a well-known Liberian lady, whose home they would ransack before daybreak in search of her husband. As it happened, I had already relocated her at our WARDA official residence. Her husband was also out of the country. My episode was thus transformed from a traumatic experience to "a happy ending."

All names have been deliberately omitted from these incidents in view of the ferocity and ugly developments, both internally and internationally, which they unleashed. Upon deeper reflection, however, I could not stop wondering about the motive for President Tolbert's assassination. He is known to have launched programmes in favour of the masses, replacing their mats with mattresses, developing the interior by rotating Independence Day celebrations in provincial capitals, etc., etc. In the circumstances, it appears that the venom was not against Tolbert or his presidency but a general revolt of the indigenes against dominance by the Afro-American-Liberian minority.

Sierra Leone, with a similar population configuration of indigenes in the interior and imported citizens around the capital city, achieved the same degree of reversal by a democratic legislative process.

Unfortunately, these divisions across the continent and within our beloved Sierra Leone are not confined to indigenes against foreign arrivals. They assume, instead, an even more destructive struggle manifested in tribal units locked in deadly rivalry that is sapping the energy of the State, and neutralising hopes of developing a genuine democratic culture. It is my hope and prayer that wherever this paragraph is read throughout Africa, it will have a restraining effect on politics based on tribalism. Those of us who have been interested and concerned observers rather than active participants in politics tend to be more perceptive and more painfully aware of these dangers. We have, of course, the option of observing and suffering in silence, knowing that we have nothing to lose. The positive result of these observations will be their beneficial effect on our successors.

The WARDA experience had its other adventures and was not without its disappointments. Diplomatic experience proved useful over a period in persuading the Agriculture Ministries in Member States to release financing for our Association's administration. After six annual round trips, however, we had to review our strategy and downsize the administration. The experience of life in various Member States was a valuable addition to my catalogue of memories. With the sight of market women with babies on their backs, piles of foodstuff on their heads squatting precariously behind a scooter/okada rider, I have nothing but admiration for African womanhood. I know how an entire family's expectation for food, children's needs and, perhaps, daddy's pocket money, will depend on how much she sells at the market on that day. Returning home in time to prepare the day's meal and care for the children is only part of her day's routine. THREE CHEERS FOR AFRICAN WOMANHOOD!!! The variety of beautifully crafted artefacts in stone, wood, metal, beads, and bones was exquisite and good for tourism.

An experience I will never forget was my first attempt to reach Equatorial Guinea from Senegal. Someone trying to be very helpful directed me to the only plane flying there on alternate days. It turned out to be a one-engine flight, which I boarded reluctantly. Since I was going to arrange for our annual meeting, my sense of duty prevailed. After an hour of endless groaning and a precarious landing, four passengers (including myself) were disgorged on a non-descript airstrip in Cassamance. This was a no-man's land between Senegal and my intended destination, a terrain full of tall grass and hardly any motorable roads, frequently (so I am told) the scene of guerrilla activity in a dispute with Senegal.

Miraculously, after my fervent prayers, a skeleton of a car emerged in response to my inquiries. I cannot remember how I persuaded him to take me but he agreed to take me through the territory to open country and mercifully by Divine intervention he did not attempt any tricks. The trip was punctuated by so many mechanical problems that I could not estimate the distance, but it took us the whole day to emerge into civilization. Never did I appreciate more, throughout my travels, the significance of "All's well that ends well."

Reflecting generally on the WARDA exposure, I was overwhelmed by the spontaneous warmth of the Liberians in the city. They enjoyed spacious living and were anxious to display the benefits of their American Exposure. Skeptics wondered if it was mere showmanship, but I personally had two experiences that indicated otherwise. A female member of our social group had to travel to Accra to get married and about 15 friends travelled all the way to support her.

Although I could not go because of duty restrictions, an even greater number came by road and by air to support me at my daughter's wedding in Sierra Leone. How much more friendly can you get!

I am pleased to observe that thirty years after the financial crisis, which hastened my exit, WARDA has been able to scale down its operations but retained its identity and importance as a vital food crop research agency within the region. I congratulate and wish them survival and success.

The intervening three decades (including five years of unemployed retirement) have engaged me in four major spheres of national service for which I was probably equipped but unprepared. These will be unfolded in succeeding chapters.

14
Exit

Returning to the old familiar ways of the Civil Service should have been mere routine (new wine in an old bottle) after my international exposure at WARDA. After all, I had the experience of the Ministries of Foreign Affairs, Agriculture and Health under my belt already, but the Ministry of Mines, to which I was now assigned, turned out to be a different kettle of fish. Big Money was at the center of its operations and the players were powerful tycoons.

Six years at the West African Rice Development Association (WARDA) did not affect my attachment to the Government Service in which I was bred. It merely ignited my zeal to serve my country, re-establish my patriotic identity and earn the honest pension that my mum and other family members envisaged when they urged me to go for the civil service.

Landing in the Ministry of Mines, I had visions of diamond and gold (even without possession) as an attraction. Effectively, however, I was eventually assigned to close down the remnants of the Austro-Minerals operation at the Marampa Iron Ore Mines, find alternative operators if possible, and retire on pension.

Because of the national focus on diamonds and rutile, however, iron ore was put on the back burner, disposing of scrap metals and iron tailings. By sustaining our contacts with various potential operators, the Government was ultimately able to contract the mines years later for lucrative production.

For someone whose career had been confined to administration and diplomacy, the garb of a businessman as manager of a mining company in intensive care was ill-fitting and challenging. I welcomed the assignment, however, as it provided an opportunity to expand my professional experience.

Accepting the challenges and encouraged by my Minister, we submitted proposals for restructuring the Government Diamond Office, which was a crucial factor in maximising Government control and revenue earnings. The eventual outcome was my transfer to the most unproductive of our mining enterprises.

I was assigned as Manager of Marampa Mines, a branch of the Ministry, to preside over its dissolution under Austrominerals, while at the same time searching for any operator who could resuscitate it. Shiploads of scrap metal, old railway tracks, copperware from unserviceable generators and tailings from ore deposits became a serious cause of disagreement between Israeli speculators and local Lebanese business interests. Caught in the middle and anxious to maintain my integrity, I was relieved to go into retirement whilst the battle was still raging. On the positive side, contacts had been made with mining interests in Australia, Egypt, China, France and USA. With so much pessimism about the future of the mines, its resuscitation as a powerful sector in the national economy seems like a modern miracle. With the prospect of adding value to the primary ore being mooted and the current Local Content Policy, hopes are bound to rise for a new life at the mines. This will be such a far cry from the days when I had to procure bags of rice to offer workers for their wages.

It is worth recalling, before we leave the area, that the mines did not consist of mere dust and metals. It was also a community from everywhere, although there was healthy interaction, probably the result of shared adversity during the lean days of my tenure. There were, of course, adventures occasionally. A memorable personal experience was when our launch broke down as night enveloped the channel linking the Sierra Leone River and the wide estuary from Kissy to Tagrin. The last ferry was just returning from Lungi but our shouts could not attract their attention. Our launch was drifting into nowhere as darkness shrouded us. I sought solace in my favourite psalms, as I could offer no technical expertise. Fortunately, the launch driver and one or two technically minded passengers were able to revive our drifting machine and we arrived at Kissy terminal an hour after we were expected. Never again did we sail without a radio or life jacket.

It was a new world involving labour relations, international trade negotiations, loan agreements and other intricacies in high finance. It was exciting and, overall, satisfying to conclude my Government service career (1950-1987) as a 'mature student' in business management once more, above the level of Cashiers Assistant or the assumed title of Assistant Cashier.

Fortuitously, I left without any debts or industrial disputes and I retired from the Ministry of Mines and the Civil Service on 4 July 1987 at the statutory retirement age of 55 years.

15
Academia Revisited

My retirement coincided with a political regime that preferred to use philosophical expertise in diplomacy and vice versa. The Head of the Philosophy Department at the University was thus deployed in an ambassadorial role, while I was invited to replace him. Thus began a new career assignment in academia.

Heading a numerically small department whose assignment serviced every other department on campus was quite a task! It seems unrealistic but, in fact, we executed the following in addition to our own Department modules:

- Foundation course for all new entrants and no degree is awarded if this course, which can be repeated, is not completed before graduation.
- Course in Critical Thinking Skills for Mass Communications students
- Logic and Scientific Method for both Science and Economics Faculty students
- Philosophy of Law for Law Faculty students

In addition to all the above, we launched an interdisciplinary philosophical magazine, "SOPHIA", which unfortunately, foundered for lack of contributions from the other departments.

I take this opportunity to record my appreciation of the loyal, supportive service offered by the Rev. Father Dr. Alfred Labor, whose death is being announced even as I write this piece. He was a simple, conscientious academic and Catholic Chaplain, without whose alliance my assignment as Acting Head of the Department would have been totally ineffective.

The chance encounter with a young chap you have forgotten, who recognises and greets you with words of appreciation for your contribution to his/her education and success is infinitely gratifying. Even more fulfilling is the active commitment to the Alumni Association, which offers us a life-long opportunity to give back to the institution our time, talents and tithes as required for its sustenance. As a former Chairman of the Western Area Branch, I recall the energy we exerted to sustain the Association under the Chairmanship of Florence Dillsworth, our former Mayor of Freetown. I hope the generation that reads this will rise to that responsibility.

My lecturing appointment at Fourah Bay College was intended to be the end of my career experience. With that perception, ideas of social responsibility began to loom large in my horizon. Membership of service institutions with commitment to social responsibility, communal service and patriotic visibility presented a new attraction and manifested itself through the Rotary movement, the Freetown Dinner Club, active Freemasonry, the Cheshire Home and an active involvement in democratic governance unpolluted by political affiliation. Commitment to my church was, of course, paramount.

In Rotary, I was aware of my financial limitations to aspire for the post of District Governor, but was sufficiently dedicated to assume club presidency. Thanks also to the perceptiveness of Past District Governor, Dr. Tommy Hope; I became District Governor's Representative in Sierra Leone (on his personal recommendation) for the successive governors from Ghana and Ivory Coast. These were delightful and rewarding experiences of community service. Rotary also gave me a chance to be involved in the development of the younger generation, through the creation of a Rotaract Club for young students at the University and an Interact Club for pupils at the Albert Academy. Masonry has been fundamental in the development of the finest aspects of my identity and will continue to complement the spiritual sustenance provided by my Church.

To the amazement of myself, more than of anyone else, I survived the trial, in spite of the severe hypertension I had developed during my hectic years in charge of the Foreign Ministry.

Two incidents with my Minister, Cyril Foray, tickle me upon recollection. As we waited to board a delayed flight at Lungi, he was invited to the firing range for some target shooting. He came back beaming, only to inform me he had a wonderful time but regretted that his Permanent Secretary was not at the target spot; whereupon I promptly observed that with him pulling the trigger, the target would have been my safest spot.

Later, in New York, the municipality invited him on a helicopter tour of the city. He commandeered me to go with him during a break in the General Assembly sessions. Wonderful expectation so far, but as we awaited the helicopter, the infamous smog suddenly descended on the city, even enveloping the top of the bridges that seem to keep New York suspended. Reflecting on the danger of risking two lives, I suggested, very persuasively, that I should return to the Assembly and await his return. Cyril was not to be deceived. Laughing his head off, he accused me of cowardice and recounted a hilarious version of the incident at every opportunity. Quite honestly, he was right!

Life in academia can be routine and stereotyped and I was tempted to glide in all directions, as this was for me an extension into overtime. As realities unfolded, a sense of mission coupled with a personal attachment to Principal Prof Cyril Foray (my former Minister) made my increasing involvement beyond teaching and research inevitable.

My interest in Philosophy had aroused controversy within the Scholarship Committee because funds were limited and the relevance of the subject to a third world underdeveloped country was not clearly obvious. My supporters pleaded that if I had done well enough to be invited by the parent University, I should be encouraged. The protagonists led by H.E.B. John, Barthes Wilson and Albert Margai won the debate and so I proceeded. My mission was to establish it as an important discipline in the University and do my best to perpetuate it after I would have left, or as academic legacy.

To achieve this aim much would depend on the students. It was probably a stroke of luck that from my part-time lectures, many persisted to Final year; few went abroad for post-grad degrees and returned to lecture. By insisting on External Examiners from academic institutions (UK, Sweden, etc.) to monitor our Final Year exam questions, answers, and dissertations, the integrity of our programme was assured.

With only three lecturers to assist me, our Department's curriculum accommodated the interest of every faculty.

At the student level, there was such a glaring disparity between the contemporary culture and our student days. The current attitude is revolutionary, unconventional and undisciplined. Academicals are not worn to lectures anymore; there are no formal dinners in the dining hall, and no Fraternity clubs like the Tea Club, Areopagus, which had lecturers as Patrons/Honorary Members to reflect their standards. The Student Representative generally emerged from these groups. The modern student often dresses shabbily, speaks inaccurately and rarely completes a statement in English without some basic grammatical error. Happily, with persistent effort, the Law graduates and my Final Year students have risen above that level.

There were indeed social groups transformed into cults, whose initiation ceremonies were held in the surrounding forest after midnight and involved inhuman excesses, which sometimes necessitated criminal prosecution. Ghastly and disgraceful as some of these revelations may appear, it is necessary to bring them to the attention of succeeding generations of students if our Alma mater is to regain most, if not all, of its former glory.

A commitment on the part of both Faculty and students, based on self-respect and cooperation is necessary for salutary results. In my case, it pleases me to recall that my pre-final and final year students elected to come to my office to complete their courses when duties of State necessitated my reassignment.

Comparatively managing a Foreign Ministry and fifteen missions abroad with all the staff and supporting financial and material resources was challenging enough but my duties at the University came a close second. In addition to heading the Philosophy Department, I was appointed to act as Head of the INSTADEX Institute of Adult Education and Extramural Studies for two years. The Board of African Studies apparently needed a chairman as well and the lot fell on me. By sheer coincidence, Government appointed me Chairman of the National Tourist Board during this period when, to crown it all, I assumed the Presidency of my Rotary Club and the Presidency of the Old Pricewaleans Association.

By Divine Providence alone, I was able to achieve some successes. We built the first wall around the Prince of Whales Field; Rotary District appointed me District Governor's Representative for two incumbents and mandated me to present the first charter to the Rotary Club of Makeni. The Tourist industry was launched in international trade fairs and tourist visa fees were for the first time collected abroad and paid into a foreign bank account. The Struggle continued.

16
The View from Upstairs

The problem with the labyrinth is how to get out. Getting in is so easy. This seems to have been my experience in gliding from one occupation to the next during my entire career. I readily recall the sudden and unexpected transition from provincial administration to diplomatic trainee and the vista of a brand new world. An invitation to academia during my penultimate year of civil service tenure also fits the pattern easily. Leaving academia was no different.

President Kabbah was elected into his first term during my penultimate year of University lecturing (1996) and reportedly sent for me the next day. Being fully engaged and on campus whilst his distinguished emissaries, Solomon Berewa and Gervas Betts, were occupied in designing the future, I was only discovered four days later and immediately given an assignment at State House.

It turned out that he wanted me to set up a unit at State House similar to what Sylvia Blyden did for President Koroma but without the media component. Anti-corruption was his target and I was to create a Unit within State House as a nucleus. In view of the President's well-known reluctance to commit Government funds, my assignment was referred to the UNDP, which recruited and posted me to State House whilst funding all my supporting expenses. The British High Commission and the British Council augmented the effort providing some office furniture, a library of anti-corruption literature and funding for Anti-corruption training, which I pursued for two weeks each at the Economic Crimes Commission in Botswana and the Royal Institute for Public Administration in London. The Unit for Monitoring Accountability and Transparency (UMAT), which I established, was destroyed by the coupists, but my surprise is that after all that experience and training, including observation tours in Uganda and a Conference in Cambridge, my connection with that important state organ was completely ignored after President Kabbah's exit, even though top level officials at State House were alerted as I retired from the National Commission for Democracy (NCD).

From this emerged the foundation of an Anti-Corruption Unit, which I labeled "Unit for Monitoring Accountability and Transparency (UMAT)". Thanks to the active support of the British Government and the United Nations Development Programme, it was sufficiently influential to earn me the doubtful accolade of "Kabbah's Bloodhound" plus an enviable contract as a UNDP staff member. Alongside Dr. J. S. Forna as Economic Adviser, I was also Special Executive Adviser and Director of UMAT.

The destruction of my office among others at State House was one of the catastrophic outcomes of the onslaught on that establishment on May 25 1997. It was disturbing to realise that even a rudimentary anti-corruption entity was such a hateful reproach to potential, aspiring leaders of our nation.

Fortuitously, the American Ambassador had issued me a ticket and special visa the previous week for a leadership observation tour of the USA. My travel allowance was to be collected on the day after the coup but in the prevailing circumstance, the lack of money was of little consequence. My arrival in New York the following week was the beginning of a year in exile, diplomatically overlooked by the State Department but not financially supported until a return ticket home was issued at my request.

At State House, it was liberating to be housed in a separate building, free from the weight of interactive tension and oppressive space constraint. On the other hand, I was easily accessible but I regulated unnecessary intrusion. Since I had unrestricted access to His Excellency out of the office, there was no need to impose myself on him in the office except as absolutely necessary. There was moreover, not much time to be spent in the office as I felt it necessary to be present at every central Procurement Committee meeting in addition to a variety of Board meetings, especially those that were considered crucial to national development. These included the Bank of Sierra Leone, Sierra Leone Airways, and Sierra Leone Ports Authority. My interventions, seen as State House input, were well received but never imposed and results were regularly reported back to His Excellency. Out of courtesy, and to keep communication fluid, there were consultations from various quarters (MDAs) and this really facilitated the flow of my work, even if it was sometimes complicated enough to almost frustrate my diplomatic skills.

Presumably, out of concern for my welfare, or sometimes as a temptation, I was offered a sitting fee, but not being a member of the Board and only an observer, I was content to share their tea and snacks but NEVER accepted an allowance.

State house had its glamour and pitfalls. His Excellency made no secret of his confidence in me and my performance. I can even recall him confessing that he often thought it necessary to seek my reaction because he trusted my analysis and judgement. This was flattering but very uncomfortable as it made many state officials less friendly. This awareness did not discourage me, however, as I was always confident that he would protect my independence. Because of our frankness towards each other, there were moments of disagreement over strategy, if non-substantial

122

matters were referred to me. Being the boss and more strong-willed than I am, he listened well, but made his own decisions. It was an ideal situation. Nevertheless, I appreciated his confidence, which displeased some. An outstanding example was when he was proceeding to sign the Lomé Agreement. I was then in the NCDHR, facilitating the participation of Civil Society with UNDP assistance, as my Chairperson Dr. Kadi Sesay had proceeded ahead. To my surprise and pleasure, he invited me to join his special flight offered by the Nigerian Government. There were some already asserting unspecified rights to be there. They were allowed to go but I cannot recall them returning with us. I only hope they found justification of my trip when I spent several weeks translating and explaining the entire Agreement in Krio to the nation.

On the return trip, I was sitting unobtrusively at the rear end of the plane when a summons rather than an invitation was issued for me to join him. My first reaction was one of elation, only to realise that he was to travel to the U.K. in a day or two and wanted a proposal for a Commonwealth special assistance. It was work, work, and work for me all the way back but the favourable outcome of that proposal and its lasting effect on the Presidency (both of himself and his successor) have amply rewarded my sense of duty as well as my political impartiality. I hasten to add that I draw a clear distinction between impartiality and neutrality. There must be many readers wondering about this nebulous outcome, which has benefitted two Presidents to the extent that I cannot resist mentioning it. It is the outstanding quality of State protocol, which resulted from that exercise. My product was not just for President Kabbah but also for State House.

17
Democracy and Human Rights

People with a humble beginning tend to have great respect for egalitarian ideas and the rights of others. They readily embrace movements advocating or sponsoring participation by masses, especially the underclass including themselves, in the belief that the greatest good flows from "each for all and all for each." However, believing and acting on the maxim often involves delays and mobilisation strategies that may ultimately result in stillbirth.

It is possible that I had traces of that streak but I never initiated any action in that direction. Rather surprising, it must have been for the populations as it was for me, that it was a military Head of State, generically dictatorial, who established the National Commission for Democracy and Human Rights. The lady who was appointed as Chairperson had been a colleague on the University staff and to my surprise, she invited me to undertake the radio aspect of the Commission's public relations programme. Thus began a professional engagement with the Commission; first as a Gratuitous Consultant and later as a regular staff member until the end of my working life.

The Commission, to my mind, had as its major motivations to popularise awareness of democracy as a positively socio-political culture and devise programmes to spread that idea nationwide--to the rulers and the governed alike. This represented a significant change in the political culture locally. In the past, democracy was practised as a confrontational conversation, involving inter and intraparty opponents, Government and the Opposition at each other's throats, Civil Society as blood hounds after Government rather than mediators and regulators; with spices of tribalism thrown into the cauldron culminating in an explosive eruption during the litmus test of "democratic" elections.

Chair of NCD and team presenting final report to the President

It was not easy to change this culture, which was simplistically linked to the colonial paradigm of Government and Opposition. Over there, Governments operate under the constant awareness that the electorate will determine their fate by their performance.

During my tenure both as an unpaid consultant and later as a staff member, our consuming passion was to transform the image of democracy from negative to positive. In this perspective, the political conversation was to be inclusive rather than divisive. Discourse should be less confrontational and decisions in the public interest more consensual. The Constitution was presented not as an Instrument of Power for the rulers but as a foundation of the rights, privileges, and obligations of every citizen towards the State. In essence, it was intended and designed to consolidate good citizenship and patriotism. We even proposed the emphasis of Majority and Minority parties within a unified Parliament in preference to Government and Opposition.

One is aware that old habits (especially bad ones) die hard and many of our dreams are still unrealised. I am hopeful that a generation will eventually emerge from the attitudinal and behavioral change campaign whose vision will extend beyond the present and the past to lay new pathways for the positive aspects of democratic governance, which will make Sierra Leone a light house in the navigation of the democratic experiment. It seems to me that one of the problems encumbering the concept of democracy is the attempt to present it as a simplistic formula applicable to all cultures everywhere. This paradigm needs to be reviewed to make room for cultural heritage and maximal benefits (e.g. community survival, material resources distribution). In this way, different specific elements of the democratic concept become relevant and useful to specific societies, avoiding the confusion of "One size fits all" without straying from the encompassing umbrella of "Government of the people, by the people, for the people."

Injecting a new culture into our system was complicated by the high degree of illiteracy or semi-illiteracy in English, the official language and the language of basic education. There was also sensitivity of minor languages to be considered. Pictorial images, postcards, drama and workshops in local languages and interactive meetings with all levels of local communities yielded recognisable dividends. Most important was the invaluable collaboration of parallel institutions whose mandates and objectives were clearly within the ambit of cultivating democracy. These included the National Election Commission under the distinguished leadership of Dr. Christiana Thorpe, The Political Parties Registration Commission, Human Rights Commission and the Inter-Religious Council. In my later years, we were able to form a new group comprising all these members plus Civil Society, which operated under the umbrella of the National Commission for Democracy, with the nomenclature of Moral Guarantors led by Mrs. Agnes Taylor-Lewis. The guarantors were mandated to identify and address emerging threats to the nation's peace and tranquility.

Styles of management may change with the injection of new personnel, but the Commission, which produced the National Pledge to emphasise every citizen's commitment to the National Anthem, will have a continuing role to play in sustaining democracy in Sierra Leone through civic education in and out of the classroom. This is a wakeup call to go back to the comprehensive civic education programme for various levels in schools, backed by Awareness Raising clubs, which initiated and sustained pupil interest in patriotic and national affairs. Of all my national duties, the NCDHR was probably the most comprehensive through its effects on virtually every aspect of our lives as a nation and as individuals. The primary focus at the Commission's inception was to awaken the consciousness of a sleeping population, largely illiterate to their role as active participants, in a new democratic process. Our challenges included designing, packaging, transmitting and sustaining our message within communities insulated by traditional cultural customs and norms. Assigning equal rights and privileges to all men, women and eventually children was perceived as a devastating assault on the security of their parochial world.

Our strategy was to engage partners who were relevant to peculiar assignments and work simultaneously in all the regions and districts for maximum nationwide effect. The National Democratic Institute (NDI), the UN family, International Non-Governmental

Organisations (INGOS), the 50/50 Women's Advocacy Group and the Inter-Religious Council were significant supporters to the core alliance we had forged. This included many organisations, such as the U. N. Human Rights Commission in Geneva, the local democratic institutions in charge of the elections (NEC, Political Parties Registration Commission (PPRC), Civil Society organs like Campaign for Good Governance, the security forces and the media, in which I became an inevitable role player. The profile of the Commission catapulted into some very demanding assignments, especially after I was elevated from Commissioner to Chairman, when our human rights component had also acquired enough stature to be assigned to a separate commission. Relieved of that assignment, I became a regular choice to chair almost every national meeting connected with elections and the democratic process. I was thus able to interview all twelve candidates, including the late President Ahmad Tejan Kabbah, for the 1996 general elections. My emphasis on anti-corruption at that interview may have influenced him to invite me to State House, where I designed and directed the Unit for Monitoring Accountability and Transparency (UMAT). With that experience behind me, I was not surprised to be invited to chair the 2008 Presidential debate, where the only absentee was Mr. Solomon Berewa, the eventual runner up. When uncertainty loomed over the prospect of a peaceful transition in that race, we hastily formed a peaceful transition committee with Bishop J Humper as Chair, but again, I was profiled as the committee's media spokesperson. Meeting together even on Sundays after service, we can claim a measure of success in the smoothness of that transition.

Other major activities of the commission included:

- Taking local government to the people and sensitising the chiefs and elders to facilitate change in their communities
- Distribution of leaflets, postcards, etc. as personal mementos
- Producing the national pledge and ensuring that it was regularly sung in all schools
- The preparation of an abridged version of the constitution
- Publicising the national symbols, i.e. the National Anthem, the National Flag and Coat of Arms, through publications and lectures
- Holding workshops for parents and children separately on the Convention on the Rights of the Child
- Most important were our regular sensitisation seminars, after every General Election, mainly for new Parliamentarians

Although these activities cover a significant volume of our work, two very important issues will persist and survive as indelible legacies with me for all time.

The first was the message of the late president, Alhaji Dr. Ahmad Tejan Kabbah, on the need for peace, forgiveness and reconciliation after the civil war. Guided by this message, one of my most memorable achievements was at a workshop where I succeeded in getting Mr. Moiwo of the Liberation Forces and Eldred Collins of the RUF to embrace publicly in front of television cameras as an act of reconciliation.

The second was the idea of attitudinal and behaviorial change, which emerged from a discussion between His Excellency the President, Dr. Ernest Bai Koroma, and me as Chair of NCD in the early days of his accession to the Presidency.

If both ideas are pursued with diligence and dedication, our dearly beloved country cannot but prosper.

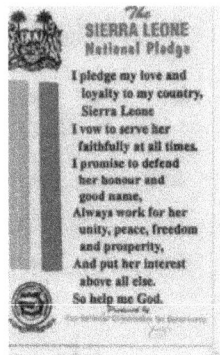

National Pledge

Democracy in view

18
Rite of Passage

I can now reveal that two major motivations dominated my endeavors. One was an obligation to reward my country for its invaluable contribution to my personal development by funding or facilitating my education. Beyond primary through secondary school in Sierra Leone, college in U.K., and special professional training in Australia and the USA, my Sierra Leonean identity, backed, of course, by my personal efforts, was the foundation of my professional activities.

The second obsession was to raise a family under conditions more favourable than my own, thus defacing the past and constructing for my offspring an ideal model for themselves and their succeeding generations.

This Rite of Passage is a brief excursion into the unusual and rather unorthodox methods used to realise my second objective. I do not apologise for my modus operandi because they were well-intentioned and apparently succeeded. Let me hasten to add however that I did not have to go it alone. My partner, Olivia, ably assisted me.

Among our offsprings......

- Daisy obtained a US degree, taught in the premier Girls Secondary School in Freetown before relocating to the UK as a teacher and social worker.
- Georgia, who was lacrosse captain in St. Elphines in England, studied both Pharmacy and Mathematics,

and has lectured in U.K. Colleges throughout her career.

- Anne obtained her doctoral degree in the U.S., where she is now a tenured Associate Professor in Human Resource and Management.
- Helen (unfortunately deceased) obtained the highest level Certificate in Tourism and Travel, her chosen discipline.
- Marion is a practicing Solicitor in London.
- Grace is a practicing Barrister and Solicitor in London and Sierra Leone.
- Coretta teaches English and French in the US while pursuing a higher degree.
- Glenna runs a secretarial unit in a US medical facility.
- Martha Georgina was the latest addition to my brood after all my others had left the roost and relocated abroad to pursue and consolidate their individual fortunes. This was my period of greatest need of home service, care and support. Being a minor in need of further education, we were gaining from each other. For now and always, she is my latest daughter, loyal, serviceable and very supportive. May God protect and prosper her especially in my absence.

I would like to believe their earlier exposure in life prepared them for their achievements. Whenever it was convenient, we enrolled them for ballet classes, music, Girl Guides, brownie groups as well as religious instruction.

They also benefitted from exposure to the best elementary and secondary schools: the Ridge Church School in Ghana, Annie Walsh, St Joseph's, Fourah Bay College Primary, Bertha Conton Elementary in Sierra Leone, UN School and Montessori in New York.

All gratitude must be given to the Most High who made all this possible.

Although fate separated Olivia from me physically and eventually by death, we were never spiritually divided; we always acted together on any matter affecting the children.

Bless them all for the wonderful gifts of numerous grandchildren and great grandchildren with which they have beautified my life and extended my line.

Being married before we were officially qualified at 21 years of age and relying on no resources except insecure low-level jobs and a determination to succeed sounds adventurous. So it is, and therefore I DO NOT RECOMMEND IT TO ANY YOUNG MAN.

19
The Twilight

Transition and Transformation, however long and complex, come to a halt in the twilight. This is the moment when the hopes and fears, the struggles, successes and failures of all the years come home to roost; and when Time and Eternity converge in interactive revelation, evaluating the synthesis. Moments of regret over missed, mistaken or misused opportunities are illuminated by memories of heroic adventures over obstacles. Sacrifices in the interest of others rank high in such reckoning. In contemporary imagery, this is the essence of the transit lounge. It is a state of patiently expecting but not necessarily waiting for the end knowing it will come when it must come.

Lest we sink into melancholy and depression, it is advisable to capture some of the reassuring features of the twilight zone. First, we must not stumble on to it. It should be anticipated as a goal of one's lifetime. As the saying goes, "As we begin to live we begin to die." Our twilight therefore starts with our moment of conscious activity. Our final moments, therefore, do not or should not descend upon us unawares. From transition through transformation, we are the major contributors to our ultimate identity. Awareness of this fact makes twilight an inspiration and our obligatory goal.

Does it not also strike us that the glorious Sun, in its daily apparent journey across the sky, reserves its most majestic display for the exotic beauty of the twilight hour? Let us conceptualise it with the poet as "the beauty and the wonder of the world, their colours, lights and shades, changes, surprises and GOD made them all."

That is God's contribution to twilight for man's delight and inspiration. Our contribution to our own twilight is man's affirmation of his claim to divinity.

20
Epilogue

As my activities in the Church and Masonic circles are expressions of my intrinsic relationship with my God and my fellow creatures, I have decided, out of modesty, to indicate that I was very committed in both areas where I was privileged to attain the highest levels of trust and responsibility and did my best to further the interests of the less privileged colleagues and the youth.

If the narrative proves tedious or incomplete, blame it on my human frailty and incompetence. If you want more, consult me before my twilight fades. I hope this affirmation of mutual commitment will reassure those who tend to perceive a dichotomy between the Church and the Masonry. At a certain point in my transformation, I was almost distracted by an apparent conflict between my religion and my philosophical studies. My solution was to distinguish between faith as the basis of religion and certain knowledge which philosophy offers, especially in logic. I sincerely recommend religious and masonic values in conjunction with our rigorous academic discoveries.

District Grand Lodge Team including Past District Grand Master (D.G.M.) Dr. Willoughby and myself as deputy D.G.M.

21

The 2005 Wilberforce Lecture

Challenges Confronting Democracy in Africa Introduction

The following is the edited recording of the Wilberforce Public Lecture at the Guildhall, Alfred Gelder Street, Kingston-Upon-Hull on Monday 24 October, 2005. George Coleridge-Taylor, who has spent his life working towards democracy in war-torn Sierra Leone, delivered the lecture, entitled "Challenges Confronting Democracy in Africa, the Sierra Leone Experience". His previous positions have included Acting High Commissioner in Nigeria during the Civil War of 1968-69 and Permanent Secretary, Ministry of Mines, 1984-87. At the time of this lecture, he held the position of Chairman of the National Commission for Democracy and Human Rights.

Chair:

[Applause]. Good evening ladies and gentlemen. Welcome to the Wilberforce Lecture. It gives me great pleasure to introduce the Chairman of the Freetown Society, Honorary Alderman Dr. Patrick Doyle, and Member of the Order of the Republic of Sierra Leone. Dr. Doyle. [Applause]

Dr. Patrick Doyle:

Deputy Lord Mayor, Your Excellency, Mr. Mayor, Councilors of Kingston-Upon-Hull and Freetown, Ladies and Gentlemen, a special welcome to George Coleridge-Taylor, and a little apology if I take some time over the introduction. It is for a reason. This is a Wilberforce Lecture, and it is very appropriate that someone from Freetown, Sierra Leone, should give it. There is a twinning between the city of Freetown and Wilberforce, as Wilberforce and his colleagues were instrumental in establishing the free colony of Sierra Leone in the late 18th century; and, indeed, there is a village in Sierra Leone called Wilberforce. And, shortly after that, one of the first Governors of Freetown was another former Hull Grammar School boy, Perronet Thompson. However, I want to speak for a moment about another link, and you will see the reason why.

The observant amongst you will notice that George and I are wearing the same tie, and that is because we were at the same college at Durham many, many years ago. So, my first memory of George is of a young distinguished orator who, within a few weeks of being at college, we elected onto the Durham Union Committee and later, before graduation, George became President of the Union. Therefore, he has always been a good speaker, and he has been an academic and a diplomat. But that link between Durham and Fourah Bay is important, because in those days, Fourah Bay was a constituent college of, or affiliated to, Durham. The degrees of Fourah Bay were Durham degrees, and amongst an older generation in Freetown, they still speak about being of the Durham breed, meaning receiving a Durham degree.

Now, amongst the lecturers at Durham was one Leo Blair. He was instrumental in setting up the law school at Fourah Bay, which is one of the reasons why his son has taken such a close interest in Sierra Leone affairs. In 2000, Mr. Blair was speaking in Hull. During that time, the then Mayor of Freetown, Henry Ferguson, was with us. Regrettably, a Yorkshire soldier had been killed in Sierra Leone, and Mr. Blair, unscripted, realising that Mr. Ferguson was present, spoke about this. He said something I thought was important at the time-- that he would not stand by and watch the fledgling democracy in Sierra Leone die. And democracy is the subject of George's talk tonight.

The last time I met George, he had a great shock of grey hair and a great grey beard. He looked, in African style, a man of great wisdom, which he is. Therefore, I was surprised when I saw him yesterday, shorn of his locks and shorn of his beard. I was happy when he said to my colleague when we were on a delegation to Freetown, pointing to me, "That man when he was young was a radical in Durham." It did not take much to be a radical in Durham in the 1950s. And then he said, "He brought people like Barbara Castle to Durham," which was true; but when Barbara Castle came to Durham, she came to speak to the Labour Club, which is true; but she spoke on behalf of the Movement for Colonial Freedom. Just think about that. It was The Movement for Colonial Freedom, Fenner Brockway's organization. This is because when George was at Durham, Sierra Leone was still a colony of Britain. It had not yet reached independence. This all hangs together, you will see in a moment.

Well, you see, the link between Hull and Freetown, which is why we are here tonight in one sense and why we are celebrating 25 years of the link, is such that those close observers of the Sierra Leone scene realised that matters would implode unless something was done. Any observer of Sierra Leone affairs could see something was going to happen and, throughout the late eighties and nineties, some of us were writing to the then government, people like Baroness Chalker, pleading for intervention, pleading for help and assistance. We received the same message; the place is riddled with corruption, sort that out and we'll help. Nothing was done and the inevitable followed. However, we the Freetown Society even in the darkest of days, still managed to get rice supplies into a rice kitchen in Kissy; we still managed to get medical supplies through Médicins sans Frontièrs into the hospitals in Freetown even when the rebels were in parts of the city.

And when the new government came to power and decided to intervene, the then High Commissioner, Peter Penfold, who his Excellency told me was made a Paramount Chief, another subject George will refer to later on, for the sterling work he did in helping to restore law and order in Freetown and beyond. Peter Penfold came to Hull and met with John McSharry, who is here tonight with me to talk about Sierra Leone affairs. Such was the paucity of knowledge about Sierra Leone and the Foreign Office that came here and, to our surprise, a fortnight later we had a telephone call from what I used to call the War Office, Ministry of Defense, and two Military Intelligence Officers came out to see us to ask about Sierra Leone. That was quite interesting.

You see, George has lived through independence; he has lived through multiparty democracy, a one-party state, military coups, military dictatorship, chaos, civil war, violence even in the heart of the capital, and lived to see the restoration of multiparty democracy. He has seen it all. However, he has seen it through the eyes of an academic. He has also seen it through the eyes of a diplomat, having been a member of the Sierra Leone Foreign Office and served as a Special Envoy and with the United Nations. I have not told you what his special field of academic study is. He is a philosopher. A philosopher. So he brings the wisdom of Africa, he brings philosophy, he brings a wealth of experience as a diplomat, an envoy, and as an academic who is not retired – he tells me he is returning to Freetown soon to continue lecturing at Fourah Bay.

And that was probably the reason why when they were looking for someone in Sierra Leone to head the National Commission for Human Rights and Democracy, to look at and explore reconciliation on the same model as Archbishop Tutu in South Africa, they turned to George Coleridge-Taylor and invited him to act as Chairman of that Commission. That, I suggest tonight, is a measure of the man. He is a man who has seen it all, lived through it and retained his integrity, retained his model integrity, so that he was the man who was given the task of looking after that Commission.

I say no more. I invite George Coleridge-Taylor to address you on this important subject of democracy in Africa and, when he is finished, he will be pleased to answer questions on what he has said and to answer questions on his role in charge of this Commission on human rights and democracy in his country. It is my great pleasure to invite George to address you now.

Coleridge-Taylor delivering the Wilberforce Lecture at the Guild Hall, Kingston-Upon-Hull, U.K. 2005.

George Coleridge-Taylor:

Mr. Chairman, your Excellency, the High Commissioner for Sierra Leone in the United Kingdom, your Worships the Deputy Lord Mayor of Kingston-Upon-Hull and the Mayor of Freetown, Honorable Members of the Wilberforce Committee as well as the Freetown Committee, distinguished – obviously Distinguished Ladies and Gentlemen, please allow me first of all to acknowledge the very flattering, even if not completely accurate, introduction, generously but I am sure genuinely lavished on me by the Honourable Alderman and Chairman of the Freetown Committee, Patrick Doyle. The generosity of his compliments certainly deserves my thanks. As he progressed, however, I have to confess I did pinch myself for reassurance because back home such copious compliments are reserved for the deceased at funerals.

Actually, Alderman Doyle, I was impressed by your discretion in not disclosing that I have upset the gender balance in my home country by adding nine daughters and no sons to the population. Happily, my daughters have redressed the balance by bringing me sons-in-law, one of whom is here present accompanying two of my daughters. On their behalf and in my own name, I express sincere gratitude for the warm welcome and generous hospitality we are enjoying as the guests of the municipality of Kingston-Upon-Hull and the Wilberforce Committee. May I also use this opportunity to acknowledge publicly how gratified and honoured I am by this felicitous privilege of delivering the 2005 Wilberforce Lecture on the kind invitation, again, of the municipality and the Wilberforce Committee. I trust that as we proceed, if any variations should emerge in our perceptions of democracy, they will only help to strengthen the bonds of freedom that have always united our two nations and our two municipalities across cultural divides.

I shall be more than a little gratified if some of my ideas generate or revive some debate that will enhance our perceptions and understanding of democracy and the values that democracy may impart. In making this presentation, it is also my hope and intention to stimulate the interest and sympathy of friends and patrons in Britain, the world beyond, and not least my fellow compatriots. It is appropriate at this point to acknowledge with gratitude the philanthropic inspiration of William Wilberforce, whose lofty motivation for freedom, human freedom, resulted in the act banning the British slave trade. Not content with this achievement, he sought to ensure the safety of rescued victims by establishing the Province of Freedom, which covers present day Freetown and surrounding villages. His partners in this venture, Clarkson, Sharp, Fox, and Granville also deserve our commendation, but it is mainly to his vision that we owe the Sierra Leone of today.

As a Commissioner for Democracy in the developing state of Sierra Leone, I am aware that the reputation and image of my country between 1991 and 2002 were derived from its assassination of most of the attributes of modern democracy. The image that many of you may currently hold of Sierra Leone is one of a war-torn African nation devoid of humanity, where amputees bear the scars of political failure. It is somewhat inevitable, therefore, that my choice of topic for this lecture revolves around the theme of democracy in an African environment focusing on the Sierra Leone experience. I actually preferred democracy and an African culture, but it savoured too much of … philosophy and an African culture. I therefore settle for second best.

"Challenges confronting democracy in Africa, the Sierra Leone experience." In the first place, although democracy has become a new household word in many societies across continents, there is an obvious need expressed in each of its contexts for further clarification to facilitate acceptance or rejection of democracy in its modern dress. Secondly, I would wish to show that some form of democracy predated the prepackaged variety now advertised, recommended, and prescribed as a universal panacea. It should be helpful to examine and explain the differences especially as a feature among the challenges, and to see whether it is desirable to marry the old and new varieties of the concept into a model of democracy that can be easily digested by African tradition.

The world we have inherited reflects such political and cultural diversity, economic inequity, and intellectual fervour that it is difficult to present any concept in a manner that will be uniformly understood and accepted universally. We may, therefore, start by clarifying the central concept in this presentation, which is democracy. When President Gorbachev veered hesitantly into the open society, he hardly envisaged a lock, stock and barrel importation of American democracy. Similarly, President Museveni of Uganda, in embracing the new democracy, had to choose between democratic pluralism, liberalism, and no party democracy. In Sierra Leone, the native intelligence of our late President, Siaka Stevens, was never more vivid than when he tried to defend his one-party state by equating it with a democracy in which everyone was participating collaboratively rather than through confrontational parties. The obvious flaw in that presentation is that the collaboration was not voluntary but legislated and compulsory.

There is, of course, the Y2K version made in the new world, patented in Europe, highly priced, and equally prized, and advertised worldwide as a product of the global village with a harmless Irish claim that it, like Guinness, is good for you. It is harmless, of course, until you imbibe too much in a distant Palaver Hut. Experience suggests that prepackaged democracy may be inappropriate. It is best unwrapped or adulterated to suit the local constitution and persuasively dispensed in order to be not just acceptable but even palatable. It may otherwise result in a convulsion and, even where the draft is home brewed, too much too soon can be lethal.

The French Revolution and the very local experience of Cromwell's enterprise are, to my mind, obvious examples of important local medication taken in overdose. Although both events appeared to pursue the identical objective of eliminating aristocratic and oligarchic rule, neither was completely successful in that sense, not until the current millennium when the aristocracy has apparently lost its political clout in England. As for France, it is difficult to see fraternity germinating from the guillotine. It is even more difficult to imagine pervasive egalitarian liberty flourishing in the fratricidal environment of the revolution. Objectivity and contextual realities, however, dictate caution in the rush to resolve in less than half a century some of the problems with which the more established democracies are still grappling after centuries of trial and improvement. Did it not take the British generations to grant women the vote? Well, within 44 years, Sierra Leone is already vigorously pursuing a 50/50 gender goal in virtually every social, political and economic department in governance. A Deputy Speaker of Parliament, a distinguished elected lady, acted as Head of State while the current minority leader of the house as I write, Dr. Bernadette Lahai, is another dynamic lady.

Another significant proof that democratic doctrines are bearing early fruit was the slogan adopted by Bai Bureh, the Temne warrior for his hut tax war in 1898: No taxation without representation. Equally interesting were the perceptions of democracy arising out of that dispute. While the Creole sense of justice supported the slogan as a democratic maxim, the British Administration thought the Creole fervour was misguided by too much democracy. To quote from the Governor's dispatch of May1898, he was, and I quote, "…..hampered with a large community of half educated people who have had free institutions given them which they cannot use aright, and the liberty of the press, which has degenerated into license."

He goes on,

> "Freetown's sympathy was openly expressed for Bai Bureh and his cause. Prayer meetings were ostentatiously held by the mammies, or market women, for his conversion, and the first of such meetings was inaugurated outside Government House."

Freetown was a brand new settlement composed of disparate persons from diverse though related cultural backgrounds. It was a heterogeneous group of interests, bound together by the imperative of survival. For such a crowd to have built a city; organised a municipality, however flawed; cultivated a transplanted religion to maturity in an environment already invaded by the powerful rival force of Islam; established a press free enough to be accused of license; and imbibed democratic principles sufficiently to use them against their tutors, all these attest to the remarkable capability of that new breed, the new Sierra Leonean. Theirs is a potent mixture

147

of receptiveness and innovation. In the context of our discourse, it also testifies to the fact that democracy of a sort had fallen on good ground in Sierra Leone over a century ago.

The agitation of the citizens, including public demonstrations, by the mammies, buttressed by a free press clamouring for the right of representation could well have been a story in today's media. Bai Bureh's rebellion indeed advocated two principles central to our modern democratic codes. These are, on the one hand, participation through representation and, on the other, responsible citizenship. After all, he did not oppose taxation but only taxation without representation. In the process of cultural or ideological interaction, dominant strains tend to influence the direction in which the weaker ones develop. The British influence within the province did not have a smooth ride, however, because one of the counteracting forces was the indigenous local culture, robust and aggressive in its own right. But in local tradition, culture embraced politics as well as religion and economics and, as the profile of that culture increased among the newly freed settlers, the stronger became their political resistance to management by the colonial rulers.

Taking a backward glance at their various backgrounds, we see a sound and solid system of traditional rule reflecting elements of the cultures represented in the province. The prevalent communalistic social system bonded the communities internally, although this was mostly on tribal grounds. The imperative of survival in hostile and unfamiliar territory, however, united the various groups by the familiar philosophy of united we stand, divided we fall. It is only fair to observe at this juncture that the resistance to colonial politics did not rise to the forefront until the merchants of the Sierra Leone Company, and eventually the British Crown, had succeeded the philanthropists. The philanthropists and

148

the early settlers shared a mutual interest in survival against hostile tribes, unfamiliar territory, and limited resources. Democratisation was not a priority when the imported administration and the traditional system interacted initially because the democratisation process would have caused upheavals in the social, political, and cultural heritage of the transplanted immigrants sufficient to threaten the stability of the new settlement. Transplanting a new religious doctrine in the face of traditional belief systems and the Islamic foreigner was more engaging. The founding fathers of the province were, after all, evangelists with a primary mission of Christianising their flock.

In the realm of governance, the colonial regime was more concerned with peace, stability, and external trade and, since all policy emanated from abroad, provision was only made for the locals to be involved in administration for which sufficient training was provided to make them effective and efficient assistants. The complicating factor was that some of them, like the Nova Scotians, had already experienced foreign models of government, joined the freedom train to escape from slavery, were jealously guarding their new-found freedoms and were ready to experiment with new religions and administrative systems, which they hoped would influence the hostile natives around as well as the overseas territories in the region from which many of them hailed. Because of their former exposure, they tried to blend tradition with the new political system, which would not only facilitate administration of their small ethnic communities but preserve their ethnic cultures as well.

They formed the seventeen nations at grassroots level based on immigrant groups, but this was an outstanding hybrid of the ancient and modern. Because they revolved around special cults and masquerades, however, the administrators were quite ungenerous with their blessing. As it happened, the emerging local aristocracy was equally disdainful--so much for the peculiar instance of an interaction between the colonial contact and an imported social construct of foreigners of mixed backgrounds simultaneously confronted with unification on the one hand and experimentation with governance on the other.

Traditional administration was retained virtually intact with the colonial structure superimposed. The traditional African systems were largely uniform and consisted of hereditary chiefs in hereditary succession. In its lifelong tenure, absolute power was tempered only by a benevolent paternalism, male hegemony and unbridled domination of women and children classified and administered as chattels by customary law. Within the court barry or palaver huts, there was free and frank discussion, and it offered opportunities for critical comments but there was no formal opposition as decisions were consensual. Minorities and individuals would voluntarily conform and suspend their rights in the interest of the community, as without community their identity was incomplete.

Transparency and accountability were a non-concept as the culture made no such requirements. Too much probing would erode the mystique of the ruler--such was the culture of the traditional political regime across the expanse of sub-Saharan Africa when colonialism breached its innocence.

Relying on Sierra Leone's colonial experience and my personal involvement with all of West Africa and beyond, I am led to conclude that, with the possible exceptions of Tanzania, which achieved independence without a struggle because of Julius Nyerere's non-violent philosophy, and the Francophone territories like Ivory Coast and Senegal, which were designated overseas France, the African colonies really wanted the colonialists to take leave so that they would revert to old and familiar ways without interference. In any case, the colonial hiatus did little, if anything, to entice the colonists from their ancestral politics. Significantly, it failed to introduce them to democratic norms before presenting them with the package for application. Because they were left dangling between the familiar and the unknown, the easy choice was obvious, back to Methuselah.

To illustrate with a few examples: in colonial times there was no attempt to interfere with the hereditary succession or the permanence of the tenure, except in rare and extreme cases of dispute. Again, the practice of giving and receiving gifts officially was not interpreted as bribery or corruption. It was a traditional or customary protocol, which everyone observed. Contribution to the communal pool was generally proportionate to earnings and voluntarily made and therefore disbursement, which was invariably at the discretion of the chief, raised no need for accountability.

The benefits of governance, work, food, shelter and education, were amply provided to meet the modest needs of an agrarian society of subsistence farming families. Polygamy and the extended family provided adequate labour and food for all. Education was transmitted through rites of passage in traditional societies. Health services were dispensed through the traditional medicine man and, since they knew no better, he was adequate for their needs. Besides, since most illnesses were attributed to spirit influences, there was little more to be expected or accomplished health wise. All the same, health facilities were provided and those who were exposed made use of them.

In the area of human rights men, women, and children had their entitlements culturally assigned and communally accepted in a society firmly held together by communalism in which interpersonal or intragroup relationships provided the contextual framework for their world view and belief systems. Individual rights were secondary to the group's welfare. Perhaps because they knew differently they wanted no more.

In the area of elections, access was restricted and participation was elitist. They were unfree, unfair, and certainly undemocratic. Politics was essentially consultative and consensual, facilitating tranquility within communities but paradoxically instigating competition and inter-communal rivalry, jealousy, and conflict. The colonial regimes influenced only superficially on the psychological foundation of the traditional systems, and provided few practical examples to induce widespread or deep-rooted changes. Not only were the new settlers excluded from participation and decision-making, but also clear-cut residential and cultural suppression welcomed only a handful into an elitist foreign culture, which alienated them from their masses. So, how were they to practice the free and fair elections prescribed by modern standards? As for accountability and transparency, they were scrupulously observed by the colonial administrators, but only to the colonial headquarters and not to the local citizens. Again, this was a glaring lack of practice for their successors.

On the vexed question of life presidency, hereditary life chieftaincy would require much more than a new constitution to expel the tradition. It is too firmly entrenched in the psyche, implanted by the fireside chat and the storytelling sessions. The palaver hut was the civil society legislature, small but all-inclusive. It encouraged conformity by the minority, coupled with a respect for their rights and concerns. Checks and balances were in fact non-concepts since the chief combined in himself the duties of legislative executive and judicial leader. Emerging from this background of inherited culture and unprepared for the democratic exposure by the colonial experience, it is possible to explain and understand the similar postures of post-independence African regimes.

I hasten to say, however, that my presentation is not intended to offer any excuses for the present trends. It makes a strong case instead, first for adherence to contemporary norms with the same tenacity that the entrenched traditions inspired. Secondly, when experiences are challenged by new regimes, together they present a stronger case for revisiting some treasured morals and their underlying assumptions. We may well discover that new lamps for old can be a profitable exchange. Moving from the colonial experience into independence and the modern era of global politics, the African constituency cannot even claim the inclusive certificate of participation, yet they are expected to graduate. Well, graduate from nothing into what?

What are the fundamental imperatives of modern democracy and how do they challenge the capacity and propensity of our leaders to respond positively? If we regard democracy as a way of life rather than its popular perception as a political ideology, we must admit initially that there are inherent difficulties in changing or modifying one's way of life, especially one grounded and firmly rooted and entrenched in tradition. This is not an African peculiarity, but the relative exclusion of the Dark Continent has accentuated its conservative character. Preliterate and semiliterate societies are known to be particularly conservative in the sense of resistance to cultural change.

You may recall that I have referred earlier to certain major benchmarks, which define a democratic culture today. Popular participation or government by the people is fundamental. Elections are widely accepted as a convenient mechanism of actualising it but, for the conservative African, it challenges the idea of hereditary succession. On balance, however, properly conducted elections provide opportunities for new and hopefully refreshing leadership, particularly when the citizenry has been disenchanted. The people's right to choose is thereby validated while the competition itself evokes new ideas on governance.

It is worth noting that in societies where literacy and civic education are yet to be developed, these gaps constitute formidable obstacles to political stability and national development across the African continent, and particularly in Sierra Leone, where for more than a decade education was put on hold to make room for a gruesome conflict. There has been a glaring need for human resource development through formal and informal education, skills training, and raising of civic awareness. Neglect of female education merely accentuated the problem. One of the most hopeful signs of our national recovery today is the robust ongoing programme known as Sababu, which offers girls free primary education while it aims at providing a school in every community nationwide. As a government initiative, it is highly commendable and addresses an important human rights gap in our democratic agenda.

As a challenge, human rights requirements extend beyond an agenda perspective, although the dimension of gender violence mostly against women, economic and social discrimination as well as political exclusion place the gender issue high on the list of democratic challenges. The same disabilities apply to the youths and children, as these groups are culturally regarded as goods and chattels in spite of their numerical predominance in our societies. It is gratifying that the human rights dimension is being addressed thanks to the actions of those affected in support of government's efforts to effect legal, social, and other remedies. Sierra Leone, in particular, has established two separate Ministries to cater for Gender and Children as well as Youth and Sports.

As another item on the democratic menu, human rights can easily be perceived as an intrusive interference in the process of government. The prescriptions in international instruments like the Convention on the Elimination of All Forms of Discrimination Against Women, CEDAW, the Convention of the Rights of the Child, CRC, the Universal Declaration of Human Rights, the International Bill of Rights and other related international covenants often contravene customary laws, cultural practices, and even religious beliefs. Governments are then confronted by almost irreconcilable dilemmas, compounded by external pressures to conform or suffer economic deprivation. This in turn incurs the wrath of the people.

Because the human rights problem invariably involves encounters with the law and the justice system, it is vital that the system be sanitised. After all, the courts are safety valves for diffusing violent conflicts.

They are, thus, vital to the survival, security, and stability of the State. Meeting the challenge of injustice in a democracy requires:

- Education about rights and responsibilities,
- Insulation against temptation through adequate provision for the justice system, and,
- Equal access to justice for all.

Corruption is an obvious and primary choice when identifying issues of governance. For countries receiving aid, the twin requirements of accountability and transparency are paramount. Governments must be transparent as well as accountable to both donors and beneficiaries. Add to this the fact that in traditional rule, these concepts were neither existent nor considered necessary and you have a new challenge. The first step in meeting this challenge is to recognise its devastating effects on development and on the lives of the citizenry. The strategy of name and shame only discourages the most sensitive potential offenders, but beyond this, massive sensitisation is required to raise a corruption-free society to whom corruption will be anathema.

Given the growing trend towards modern democratic principles and practices around the continent, articulated mostly by the young and adolescent generation and the urban middle class, three rational inferences may be drawn. First, our traditional system of governance has been less than fully democratic. Second, there is a conflict of values reflected in the competing perceptions through the generation gap, the older folk wrapped in nostalgic reminiscence over the days of conservative privilege and calm stability. The restless young, on the other hand, anticipating the changing scene, agitate for speedy succession, convenient constitutional reviews, new men, new systems and a transfer of power without delay and, if necessary, without transition. I refer to transition as a process in which the old is not regarded for immediate replacement by new visionary structures, but one in which the traditional serves as a solid foundation for the construction of a new edifice. In making a case for transition, I am advocating for evolution in preference to revolution. This is an argument for partnership and building of bridges across ideological rifts and age divides.

A third inevitable inference is that a shift from traditional conservatism to a more liberal and open system of governance is not materialising in our reincarnated nations. The evidence in support of this assumption is abundant and clear. Development is progressive and therefore should be welcomed, but if the strategies and the pace of change are unplanned, unrehearsed and too speedy, the result can be destabilising and even catastrophic. The process has begun in Sierra Leone in the form of free and fair democratic elections, constitutional rule, governmental reforms, new revitalised security forces, a growing sense of patriotism, awareness in all sectors of the community of the human rights and civic responsibilities of the citizens, and the revitalising of local government. Taken together, these testify to the palpable changes that are overtaking us, but it has not always been like this.

Once upon a time, not so long ago, no one would have dared to arrest a Minister or dream of taking the Government to court. Free political association and free critical speech were risks that few could afford to take. Corruption flourished unchallenged and unchecked, and it was safe and prudent not to insist on your rights or press your claims against certain categories of persons. It was easy for the older folk to accept such a situation because our traditions facilitated it. The absolute ruler was indigenous to our culture. It provided stability but opened the door to possible abuses. This is also the case with hereditary succession as against a stipulated five-year term with a possible two-term limit. The stark truth is that our traditional practices, especially the political context, did not prepare us adequately for the kind of democratic culture that we are now inheriting.

In order to substantiate this, let us briefly examine one or two major requirements of the modern democratic process, and compare it with the traditional system of our country and continent. My contention is that our traditional practices may not have been in complete consonance with modern democracy, but there was little to prepare them for the transformation. At one of the Wilton Park Special Conferences on Good Governance in

Africa, the following were listed as essential elements of good governance:

- Multiparty democracy, implying a government and opposition established on the basis of free and fair elections
- A non-political military
- Freedom of the press
- Protection of human rights
- An efficient, transparent, and accountable public service
- An enabling environment for private enterprise.

A vital component, which looms large as an amazing gap, is good citizenship. Because the all-powerful traditional ruler symbolised a cohesive sense of community, little was done to establish the mechanisms and institutions necessary to sustain the imported democracy presented at independence. Consequently, the reversion to one party rule was virtually a psychological necessity, and no wonder it enjoyed almost total acceptance across the continent for the best part of four decades. Trapped in this parochial history on the one hand, and spurred on by prospects of visionary liberalism on the other, the case for consultations and consensus in strategising our collective destiny derives new and compelling urgency. Fortunately, consultation and consensus are integral elements in our traditional communalism.

While our traditional ruling systems did not provide for plurality of parties and a formal opposition, the colloquium in the palaver hut or Court Barry provided a heritage of exchanging opposing views, accommodating minority opinions and conducting community governance for communal benefit. It can only be hoped that in charting our way forward we can draw from this rich reservoir of accumulated experience. In our simple agrarian subsistence economies, where exchange was dictated by a need, supply and custom, accountability and transparency were undebated values mainly because they were considered irrelevant. In modern trade and commerce regulated by complex theories and sophisticated accounting systems, precision in terms of accountability and transparency is of the essence. However, the open nature of customary transactions conducted under rules informally acquired and uncritically accepted by all might well be the exemplary guide in our efforts at transparency and accountability.

In a brief time restricted presentation, it is not feasible to cover adequately all the layers of comparison and connection between complex customs, traditions, and values on the one hand and the largely unfamiliar and untried descriptions of the modern democratic process on the other. Accepting the need for change is itself a challenge. The ultimate goal of a peaceful and stable democracy in Sierra Leone forged out of frank, sincere discussion and constructive planning is certainly worth the sacrifice of some traditions.

Let me now remind you of some of the cardinal values and rights that inform and animate our culture and traditions and which can beneficially contribute to the construction of a conceptual framework for remodeling post-conflict Sierra Leone. Respect for and acceptance of authority have sometimes been regarded as sycophancy or denial of the individual's rights, but while its observance leads to stability and tranquility, the breach only causes anarchy and eventually self-destruction--a life in the well-known phrase in philosophy that is "nasty, brutish and short". Kinship and the sense of communal belonging also distinguish the African, including the Sierra Leonean. Social scientists claim that the African fulfils his individuality as part of a community; therefore, he or she is willing to make considerable sacrifices for the survival and progress of the community.

Kinship is close, loving, caring, and supportive. The demands of the extended family, for example, are accepted not as a burden but as communal responsibilities, each for all and all for each. This quality of shared expectation, responsibilities and commitment to a common civic cause if applied to the nation, must constitute the ultimate in patriotism--caring for and sharing with one another. Our modern understanding of democracy revolves around good governance, which in turn promotes the management of the State and its institutions for the benefit of the citizens. It is captured in the words of the motto of the Freetown City Council, "Salus Populi Suprema est Lex." Loosely interpreted, the delivery of the goods and services needed by the people is the essence of democratic statecraft.

Without development, of course, this obligation cannot be discharged and, since the needs gap is most crucial and glaring in most African countries, they are correspondingly in greatest need of development. Democracy and development are thus mutually supportive as far as development increases wealth and opportunities for the citizens to provide a better life for themselves, whereas a stable and functioning democracy provides a conducive environment of peace and security for business confidence, which in turn facilitates investment and the production of wealth. Of course, economic activity is no longer an internal matter for any nation. The dynamics of infrastructure weaknesses, manpower depletion through AIDS, malaria and grinding poverty compounded by the inequities of external trade and finance have internationalized *Salus Populi* for Sierra Leoneans. Economic democracy has brought in a completely new set of role players: the International Community of NGOs, donors, and other well-wishers as agents in good governance. Without them, survival is often problematic, and this has been particularly true of post-conflict Sierra Leone.

The flip side of this coin, however, seems equally problematic. They invariably come obsessed with esoteric interests, well-intentioned but disparate, and frequently out of tune with local aspirations, traditions, and culture. The NGO factor thus becomes a psychological challenge, potentially destabilising.
A rationalising strategy by governments, therefore, is necessary for the following reasons:

- to determine and prioritise the nation's needs and values since it is governments, rightly or wrongly, who carry the blame for failure,
- to compile and prune lists of agencies and align them to those needs, and
- to supervise and monitor their operations. Furthermore, to preserve national sovereignty and encourage self-development, direct execution of projects must give way to national execution and/or supervision.

Moreover, in case there are NGO members here present, I would like to repeat that: Furthermore, to preserve national sovereignty and encourage self-development, direct execution of projects must give way to national execution. Ownership and direction of national development by Government and the people will actualise the fundamental democratic principle of active participation. It facilitates also capacity building and offers a chance of developing partnerships between Government and private enterprise, as well as with external agencies. Partnerships are important to counteract the popular perception of democracy as a struggle. Its vocabulary suggests conflict and confrontation between civil society and Government, Opposition and Government, employer and employee, the old versus the young, the judiciary, executive and legislative locked in a struggle of checks and balances, with the media as hostile watchdogs over them all. Such perceptions flow often from distrust of governments, which unfortunately, are justified by experiences.

There is a need to address the causes of this distrust, but frantic external efforts to establish civil society in its present form as a source of a new and alternative government ignores the fact that the existing ills are incubated within the same society from where they are injected to pollute the body politic and spread bad governance. On this theory, in order to remedy bad governance, we must also address its causes in civil society.

I would now like to recommend to humanitarian and other benefactor agencies to pay greater attention to, and invest more in, democratic citizenship, which I mentioned earlier, if their goals are to be achieved and sustained. Democratic citizenship entails love of country, respect for constitutionality, law and order, national symbols and institutions. It requires active participation in national affairs because it is based on a positive perception of the State and a genuine desire and effort to make its systems work. Democratic citizenship accepts its responsibilities with its entitlements, and cultivates a symbiotic relationship with government from which it hopes to benefit.

A democratic citizen is cultivated through changes of attitude from dependency to self-reliance, from welfare expectation to innovative entrepreneurship, creating private wealth but respecting the sanctity of public property. Above all, the democratic citizen is not solely concerned with his or her own rights but is equally committed to recognizing and protecting the rights of others, thus renouncing the policy of exclusion. The resultant policy of inclusion facilitates and encourages partnerships in national endeavours and should be embraced. It bridges divides of gender, age, class or tribe, and is invaluable for uniting groups, not as a strategy for adversarial alliances but as a mechanism for collaborative pursuit of common national goals.

Adversarial exclusion saps the potential energy of developing States and, ironically, democracies provide fertile ground for such confrontational encounters. Democracies can be divisive, adversarial, and confrontational, and in the hands of an impatient, post-conflict population, as in Sierra Leone, full of distrust and high in expectation. The prospects could be explosive. Properly guided and cultivated, political partnerships unite government with civil society, public and private enterprises, majority and minority parties, civilians and the security forces, external agencies such as the NGOs with government, and the media in partnership with all of them for achievement of national objectives. Ideally, this situation should reflect our traditional values whilst propelling us into a future of peace and prosperity.

As Sierra Leone moves from war through peace and democracy to development, let me use this opportunity to recommend to all role players the following:

- Sympathetic understanding of the factors that inhibit Africans in general from embracing fully unedited versions of the democratic prescription.
- The creation of a democratic culture reflecting local values and fully utilising local institutions like chieftaincy, particularly as local government takes governance into traditional communities.
- To assign the highest priority to the cultivation of democratic citizenship as a complement to democratic governance as both are prerequisites for State stability.
- Building of partnerships as a post-conflict strategy and a recommended principle for the democratic experiment. Benefactors must encourage and assist governments to own and manage the democratic processes through their national institutions in partnership with other role players so that when governments fail in the future they will not plead lack of experience, as was the case during the colonial era.
- To refrain from international practices such as restrictive trade and armaments transfers, which negate well-meaning national endeavours in developing democracies.

As I conclude, fortuitously on this 68th anniversary of the founding of the United Nations, which is today, there can be no more fitting celebration, no better way of saying Happy Birthday than by appealing to citizens and nations alike to inculcate a more visible democratic culture within their organisation. In the home, the nation, and the international community, may we all resort to conflict resolution by the good old traditional African way of consultation and consensus. May the ideals of democracy find a conducive home and flourish abundantly in our various environments. While I recognise the pervasive disillusionment within many existing nominal democracies, I urge you to remember the many benefits derived from the democratic culture and so hard won by so many. Democracy should be much more than a mere slogan, but for good measure let me leave you with one slogan: Let us endeavor to make democracy our way of life.

Mr. Chairman, your Excellency, your Worships, distinguished hosts, and friends of Sierra Leone, for your patient attention and endurance, your hospitality and friendship, I say on behalf of all the Sierra Leonean visitors and in my own name, a very sincere thank you.

www.ingramcontent.com/pod-product-compliance
Lightning Source LLC
Chambersburg PA
CBHW031846090426
42741CB00005B/368